Dear Reader:

S0-CAF-453

The book you are about to read is the latest bestseller from the St. Martin's True Crime Library, the imprint *The New York Times* calls "the leader in true crime!" Each month, we offer you a fascinating account of the latest, most sensational crime that has captured the national attention. St. Martin's is the publisher of bestselling true crime author and crime journalist Kieran Crowley, who explores the dark, deadly links between a prominent Manhattan surgeon and the disappearance of his wife fifteen years earlier in THE SURGEON'S WIFE. Suzy Spencer's BREAKING POINT guides readers through the tortuous twists and turns in the case of Andrea Yates, the Houston mother who drowned her five young children in the family's bathtub. In Edgar Award-nominated DARK DREAMS, legendary FBI profiler Roy Hazelwood and bestselling crime author Stephen G. Michaud shine light on the inner workings of America's most violent and depraved murderers. In the book you now hold, STOLEN IN THE NIGHT, acclaimed author Gary C. King follows the depraved path of a kidnapper intent on tearing apart a loving family.

St. Martin's True Crime Library gives you the stories behind the headlines. Our authors take you right to the scene of the crime and into the minds of the most notorious murderers to show you what really makes them tick. St. Martin's True Crime Library paperbacks are better than the most terrifying thriller, because it's all true! The next time you want a crackling good read, make sure it's got the St. Martin's True Crime Library logo on the spine—you'll be up all night!

Charles E. Spicer

Charles E. Spicer, Jr.
Executive Editor, St. Martin's True Crime Library

STOLEN
IN THE
NIGHT

GARY C. KING

St. Martin's Paperbacks

STOLEN IN THE NIGHT

Copyright © 2007 by Gary C. King.

Cover photos of Shasta and Dylan Groene courtesy Kootenai County Sheriff's Dept./Reuters/Corbis. Cover photo of house courtesy Getty Images.

ISBN: 0-312-94205-2
EAN: 9780312-94205-2

Printed in the United States of America

St. Martin's Paperbacks edition / February 2007

St. Martin's Paperbacks are published by St. Martin's Press, 175 Fifth Avenue, New York, NY 10010.

10 9 8 7 6 5 4 3 2 1

For Teresita

ACKNOWLEDGMENTS

In addition to the usual sources that a nonfiction author would use in the writing of a book about true events, such as interviews and site visits, the following media sources were consulted for information, and attributions are made throughout the book where applicable: the *Spokesman-Review*; the *Seattle Times*; *USA Today*; the *Bismarck Tribune*; *Billings Gazette*; the *Pacific Northwest Inlander*; Fox News; CNN; MSNBC; *Globe* magazine; *The National Enquirer* and Internet sites such as http://fifthnail.blogspot.com. Dialogue used throughout the book was either obtained from a direct source, or it was based on witness statements that appeared both in the news media, some of which are listed above, and in official sources. I would like to also acknowledge the work of *Coeur d'Alene Press* staff writer Dave Turner, who carefully and painstakingly reported every detail of the Wolf Lodge murders case as it developed.

Foul deeds will rise,
Though all the earth o'erwhelm them, to men's eyes.

—WILLIAM SHAKESPEARE
Hamlet

Be not deceived; God is not mocked:
For whatsoever a man soweth,
That shall he also reap.

—Galatians, Chapter 6, Verse 7

STOLEN
IN THE
NIGHT

—PROLOGUE—

As best as police investigators from various law enforcement agencies have been able to determine, Joseph Edward Duncan III, 42 years old, a resident of Fargo, North Dakota, left nearby Becker County, Minnesota, almost immediately after someone posted his $15,000 bond there. He returned briefly to his home in Fargo, after his swift departure from Minnesota following an April 5, 2005, Becker County court hearing in which he had been charged with sexually molesting a 6-year-old boy and with attempting to molest the boy's friend. It was about this time that he apparently began making travel plans. But before leaving Fargo he needed to purchase a few items to take with him that could help him get back at society for having treated him so unfairly for his past crimes. He stopped by a Wal-Mart and purchased night-vision goggles and a video camcorder. At some point he also obtained a shotgun, shells and a claw hammer. He had plans all right, and he was determined to carry them out, no matter the cost.

Ten days later, on April 15, 2005, he rented a red Jeep Grand Cherokee in St. Paul, Minnesota. He never returned the vehicle, and the Jeep was reported stolen on May 4. Police would later learn that in the time he had the Jeep, Duncan had traveled through Missouri and gone as far south as Newton County, in the far southwestern corner of the "Show Me" state, in an area that borders Kansas, Oklahoma, and Arkansas. It was there, on April 27, 2005, that he allegedly stole a set of license plates off of a car and placed them on the Jeep. It would later become clear to the police that he was carefully planning his every move, as most sexual predators do, in this instance by disguising the vehicle before it had become necessary to do so. It must have been shortly after stealing the license plates that he had made the decision to go to Idaho.

Satisfied that he would be able to give the authorities the slip, Duncan headed north again, the exact route unknown to anyone but him, until he connected with Interstate 90, most likely either in South Dakota or Wyoming, and headed west. While it is not precisely known when Duncan entered the state of Idaho, it is generally believed that he arrived during the first week in May. It was while he was en route to Idaho that an arrest warrant was issued for him in Becker County, Minnesota, for failing to properly follow the conditions of his April 5, 2005, release and for missing a subsequent court date.

No one paid any mind to the sex offender driving the stolen Jeep with the stolen Missouri plates as he made his way west. But then, why would they? He was being careful, cold and calculating, and had given little reason for anyone to pay any attention to him.

But he would be noticed soon enough.

—CHAPTER ONE—

IDAHO—A STATE PERHAPS BEST KNOWN FOR ITS NATURAL beauty, with a topography that consists of mountains reaching elevations of eight thousand feet or more and areas, like that of Hells Canyon, where the terrain plummets to fifteen hundred feet, or Snake River Canyon, which Evil Knievel tried and failed to jump on his motorcycle. Idaho's scenery is often breathtaking, and recreational opportunities include world-class skiing, kayaking, hiking, backpacking, fishing, whitewater rafting, snowmobiling and snowboarding, to name a few. Noted outdoorsman Ernest Hemingway wrote portions of *For Whom the Bell Tolls* in Idaho, and in 1961 put a shotgun in his mouth and committed suicide there.

Idaho's motto is *Esto perpetua*, which means *It is forever*. The principal white settlements were established by the Jesuits in the early 1840s, and nowadays Idaho's family and religious values are heavily influenced by the Mormons, also known as the Church of Jesus Christ of Latter-day Saints. In 1992, U.S. Marshals, the FBI and Bureau of Alcohol, Tobacco and Firearms agents stormed the home of Randy Weaver because of firearms charges against him, and his purported affiliation with the Idaho-based white supremacy group, Aryan Nations. His wife,

Vicki Weaver, and their son, Sammy, were killed in the assault, as was the family dog; when Weaver had his day in court he was acquitted of all the major charges against him, and his case is one that many Idahoans won't let the federal government forget to this day. Even though it cost the Weavers dearly, the people of Idaho generally feel that Randy Weaver and his family were heroic for exercising their individual rights in standing up to the feds.

Liberty and freedom are very important to many of Idaho's citizens, and the state's lawmakers rarely create laws that infringe upon individual or property rights. It is also common for residents to own firearms. When all is said and done, it doesn't make much sense that a convicted child molester would make a conscious decision to travel hundreds of miles from the Midwest to a state where his past deeds, if discovered, were not likely to be readily accepted, a region whose conservative residents were not likely to put out the welcome mat and allow him to assimilate into their society. On the other hand, people there tend to mind their own business and are mistrustful of government in general. Joseph Edward Duncan III had no intention of making his past sex crimes known to the state or any of its citizens, so Idaho seemed like the perfect place for him to go to carry out his mission. That is exactly what he did, and in the process his alleged criminal actions would shock and horrify the state, stun the nation and ultimately destroy an entire family.

COEUR D'ALENE, IDAHO, LOCATED IN KOOTENAI COUNTY in the northern panhandle of the state, is an area blessed with natural beauty and a true four-season climate, with each season bringing its own unique splendor. Coeur d'Alene Lake is nearby, as is Lake Pend Oreille, and mountains add to the scenery. Early French fur traders named the lake Coeur d'Alene because they believed the local Indians were clever traders whose hearts were as sharp as a bradawl, a tool with a beveled tip used to make holes in wood for brads or screws.

It wasn't until Fort Sherman was established in 1878 that Coeur d'Alene began to grow and flourish, building its fortunes on logging, mining, fur trading and lake steamers. The town later became an important link on the transportation network linking the mining operations in the east, in Silver Valley, with the smelters that processed the mined ore. A major timber boom caused the population to increase dramatically in the early 1900s, and the small frontier town expanded into a political, business and recreational center. The expansion brought with it recognition, festivals, fairs and, later, unique restaurants and shopping malls.

The crime rate also grew, but was comparatively low when viewed alongside the rest of the nation. In 2003, the FBI recorded only 203 violent crimes, and only one of those was a homicide. The violent crime rate was 5.5 per 1,000 people; the area has an estimated population of 37,262.

Parents were not afraid to leave their children alone while they went into town to run errands. Children played outside without parental supervision, rode their bicycles wherever they wanted, and built forts in the nearby woods—kids there simply did all of the things that kids would normally do where they felt safe.

Two years later, the story of Joseph Edward Duncan

III would change the way people thought about Coeur d'Alene.

DUNCAN ARRIVED IN KOOTENAI COUNTY SOMETIME DUR-ing the second week of May 2005. It is not known precisely why he stopped in the Wolf Lodge Bay area, a quiet escape for nature lovers, lightly populated and located about 8 miles east of Coeur d'Alene, just off Interstate 90. Perhaps he had merely wanted to grab a bite to eat, or to rest for a while. At some point, however, he allegedly ended up on Frontage Road and drove past a small white house with green trim, the lower portion of which appeared to have been coated with stucco on one side. This was where the Groene and McKenzie family lived.

Witnesses later told the police that the Groene–McKenzie home was sometimes visited by strangers whose vehicles had broken down on the freeway—their house was the first home anyone looking for help would see after getting off Interstate 90 and onto Frontage Road. People said that the family was always happy to help a stranger in need.

The house, somewhat secluded and surrounded by trees, brush and low-lying hills, was approximately 150 yards down a dirt driveway from Frontage Road and made an easy target for someone bent on wrongdoing. Many have speculated that Duncan likely saw his next victims, Shasta Groene, 8, and her brother, Dylan, 9, playing outside the house in the unseasonably warm May weather, frolicking in the yard, or walking or riding their bikes along Frontage Road, perhaps waving at a passing motorist, or motioning to passing truckers to honk the air horns on their semis. Shasta had been wearing her bathing suit on at least one of the days that weekend, and it has been suggested that it was the sight of two young children playing in their swimming suits that brought Duncan's depraved sexual madness to the surface.

It is believed that he reconnoitered the area for at least a day or two until he found the perfect vantage point where he could watch the kids and their family from a distance without being easily seen, using a night-vision apparatus during the evening hours. While the exact timeframe isn't known, police believed that Duncan may have stalked the family for a few days after becoming comfortable with his surroundings. Perhaps he even followed them to town when they shopped or ran errands.

Throughout the weekend of May 13–15, Shasta and Dylan's mother, Brenda Kay Groene (pronounced "grow-knee"), 40, came and went, as did Brenda's resident boyfriend, Mark McKenzie, 37, and Shasta and Dylan's older brother, Slade, 13. On Sunday, May 15, 2005, the family drove into Coeur d'Alene to run errands, and then returned home, where they enjoyed a barbecue with some friends. The gathering went into the early evening hours before it broke up. Their friends went home, and the residents prepared to go to bed. It was the last time that anyone would remember seeing Brenda and Slade Groene and Mark McKenzie alive.

The crime that Duncan was allegedly about to commit was out of character for him. His prior victims had been children, victims who were unable to defend themselves against an adult who, though standing 6-feet, 2-inches, weighed a mere 150 pounds. Tall and lanky, he should have been an easy match for another adult, particularly one trying to defend himself.

But he had come prepared.

—CHAPTER TWO—

PRIOR TO THE BARBECUE THAT SUNDAY, A NEIGHBOR, Robert Hollingsworth, had hired 13-year-old Slade Groene to mow the grass by his driveway. However, Hollingsworth had not had the correct change to pay Slade the agreed-upon $10 for the work. He promised to stop by the boy's house the following day and pay him.

When Hollingsworth showed up with the money early Monday evening, May 16, the house appeared eerily quiet. Only a dog barked from inside. Hollingsworth honked his horn but did not immediately get out of his vehicle. Nobody came outside as they normally did when someone pulled into their driveway. When he got out of his car, Hollingsworth walked toward the small covered porch, but stopped suddenly when he saw the dark red stains near the entrance. Upon closer examination, Hollingsworth could see a significant amount of blood on the doorway and the steps, which faced west. There were no lights visible inside the house. Hollingsworth noticed that both of the family's cars were parked in their usual places, but the car doors had been left open. Suspicious and growing very concerned, Hollingsworth rushed home and called 911. It was the second time in roughly twenty-four hours that the sheriff's department had heard from him. The first time he had called to report a suspicious, apparently abandoned white pickup truck parked near his barn.

When a team of deputies from the Kootenai County Sheriff's Department arrived at 12725 East Frontage Road at 6:15 P.M., everything was just as Hollingsworth had reported. There was a considerable amount of blood on the doorway and the steps, much of it spattered. Very concerned, the deputies knocked on the door, but did not get a response. The deputies yelled for the occupants to respond, to come to the door. They walked around the house—it was built in a small clearing with one side abutting a small mountain covered with evergreen trees—and peered into windows as they checked the home's perimeter. Despite their efforts, they were unable to raise anyone inside. Based on the blood that they had seen, the deputies feared that the home's occupants might be injured and decided to enter the dwelling. Noticing that a door on the east side of the house was unlocked, they went in. The deputies were aghast at the carnage they found.

There was blood everywhere, much of it in puddles around two bodies that were sprawled on the floor. Both victims had been bound with duct tape and zip ties. The injuries appeared to be centered about the head and face of each victim. One of the victims was obviously an adolescent boy, perhaps 12 or 13 years of age, lying face down in a pool of blood. It appeared at first that he had sustained a gunshot wound to his head. A great deal of duct tape had been wrapped around his head, and was also used to bind his hands behind his back.

Next to the boy was an adult woman who appeared to

be in her early forties. She, too, was lying face down in an area between the kitchen and the living room, with a severe injury to her head. She was also lying in a large pool of blood that had apparently run out of her head. Her hands were bound behind her back with duct tape, as well as with plastic zip ties, which had also been used to bind her feet.

As the deputies made their way through the house they encountered a third victim, a bald male with facial hair who appeared to be in his late thirties or early forties, lying on the living room floor with a significant amount of blood around him. Like the victims in the kitchen, his hands and feet had been bound with duct tape and zip ties, and it appeared that he, too, had died as a result of either a gunshot wound or blunt trauma to the head.

Blood spatters were everywhere, and it would take a careful crime-scene analysis to determine conclusively whether they were consistent with beating, shooting or both. The acrid smell of congealed blood was strong, and that, along with the sight of violent death, had nauseated the deputies.

They conducted a sweep of the house to determine whether there were any more injured or deceased people in the other rooms. They noted a great deal of evidence in the form of bloody footprints, bloody handprints, blood smears and droplets of blood spatter patterns in various locations, but they did not find any other people, dead or alive. They noted the presence of several firearms stored in various locations throughout the dwelling, but none in close proximity to the victims.

Mail addressed to Brenda Groene and Mark McKenzie was found outside in the mailbox next to the road, and that, as well as information found inside the house and gathered from the neighbor who had called them to the scene, suggested that the victims were Brenda Groene and her 13-year-old son, Slade, and Brenda's boyfriend, Mark McKenzie. They were told that there were two other people who lived there, both of them children: 8-year-old Shasta Groene and her 9-year-old brother, Dylan. However, there was no sign of either of them.

DETECTIVE SERGEANT BRAD MASKELL, A SIXTEEN-YEAR veteran of the Kootenai County Sheriff's Department, was off duty and relaxing at home when he received the call at 7:20 P.M. Lieutenant Neal Robertson and another officer, Lieutenant Kim Edmondson, told him about the crime and instructed him to respond to the scene and initiate an investigation. Maskell arrived at 8 P.M., finding Sergeant Lisa Carrington, Deputy Kevin Smart, and a number of other deputies, who briefed him on what they had found. Maskell looked around the house, taking detailed notes of what he saw and what he was told by the deputies.

Maskell and the deputies sealed off the house and left the bodies as they had found them, without making any positive identification of the victims. They closed off Frontage Road in the vicinity of the house and designated it as a crime scene. Sentries were posted to stand guard throughout the night. Maskell, as well as additional homicide investigators, would return at first light with crime-scene technicians and a representative from the coroner's office.

"We're treating this as an obvious homicide," Captain

Ben Wolfinger told reporters, who had begun to show up shortly after the police activity began. Deputies kept them from getting any closer to the house, and provided them with few details.

ON MONDAY, MAY 16, 2005, LEE MCKENZIE WOOD, MARK McKenzie's mother, was at home watching the news on television when the report of a murder at Wolf Lodge flashed across the screen, along with a shot of the small white house where her son lived. Knowing that there were only two families in that area, Lee was horrified. She quickly drove to her son's home and found that Kootenai County Sheriff's Department deputies had blocked the road and cordoned off the property. She approached one of the deputies.

"There are five people in there," she said.

"No, ma'am," replied the deputy. "There are only three."

"There are five," she retorted. "Three children and two adults."

Lee and her husband, Ralph, didn't realize it yet, but the news report she saw that day would forever change both of their lives.

A few hours later, law enforcement officers arrived at her home to inform her that her son was one of the victims.

AT DAYBREAK ON TUESDAY, MAY 17, INVESTIGATORS, along with crime lab personnel, returned to the Frontage Road home. Assigned to lead the investigation, Detective Maskell and his partner, Detective Sergeant Daniel Mattos, were among the first to arrive, and they quickly made official what Maskell and the responding deputies had reported the prior evening: Three homicides of a most violent kind had occurred there.

Before the end of the first day, the dead had been positively identified as the same residents of the house tentatively identified by the deputies. Following lengthy examinations at the scene by the sheriff's department detectives and crime-lab technicians, the bodies of Brenda Kay Groene, 40, Slade Groene, 13, and Mark McKenzie, 37, were removed from the house and transported to the county morgue, where definitive autopsies would be performed. From interviews, witness statements and body temperatures of the deceased, the detectives surmised that the victims had been killed sometime either late Sunday evening, or during the morning hours of Monday.

But what had become of Shasta and Dylan? they wondered. Had they met a similar fate at another location? The investigators' first priority was finding the two missing children, hopefully alive, and then finding the person or persons responsible for committing the brutal murders.

Meanwhile, volunteers with the Kootenai County Search and Rescue Council fanned out in all directions throughout the wooded areas that surrounded the Groene–McKenzie home and Coeur d'Alene Lake. Some searched on foot, others on horseback or in all-terrain vehicles, and some used tracking dogs as well as dogs that had been specifically trained to sniff out corpses. A helicopter was also used to search from the air and, as each hour passed, additional police agencies, including the Idaho State Police and the Coeur d'Alene office of the FBI, helped canvass the area, showing Shasta and Dylan's photographs to area residents in the hope that someone had seen them. An Amber Alert was also issued nationwide for the two children, describing Dylan as 4 feet tall, 60 pounds, blue eyes and blond crew-cut hair, and Shasta as 3 feet, 10 inches tall, 40 pounds, with hazel eyes and long brown hair.

"Our main concern right now are the two children we cannot find," Kootenai County Sheriff Rocky Watson told a gathering of reporters at a planned news conference.

—CHAPTER THREE—

As DETECTIVES MASKELL AND MATTOS CONTINUED THEIR investigation, the manhunt was developing into the biggest in Kootenai County history. They had only scratched the surface, and as one day followed another they ran down one fruitless lead after another, many of which only led them in the wrong direction.

They soon learned that the Frontage Road house was owned by one of the victims, Mark Edward McKenzie. They also learned that Brenda Groene had married Steve Groene, 48 years old at the time of her death, at Big Bear Lake, California, in 1986. Brenda had been 21 at the time and Steve had been 29. They'd had five children together before divorcing in 2001, at which time Brenda moved her family to the Wolf Lodge Bay area, where she'd lived with Mark McKenzie ever since. By the time of the slayings, three of her children were still living there with her and Mark under a joint custody arrangement with Steve Groene.

Additional background information showed that Brenda had owned and operated a business called Maid to Order in which she cleaned houses on a work-for-hire basis. According to those who knew her, she would drop her children at daycare and typically work all day. However, she eventually got out of the business so that she could spend more time with her family. Those who knew her described her as a good mother.

Brenda wasn't a person without problems, though. At the time of her death, she was on probation for possession of drug paraphernalia, and she had served jail time for her conviction. She had also been ordered by the court to attend drug and alcohol counseling, but financial difficulties had prevented her from completing the programs.

Another son, Jesse Groene, 18, was in jail awaiting sentencing on a felony burglary charge at the time of the slayings. One could only wonder whether the same horrible fate that had taken the lives of the other members of his family would have befallen him, too, had he not been in jail.

Jesse Groene described his brother, Slade, as an honor-roll student who had a talent for music. He was also fond of woodworking in school, and liked the outdoors. Jesse described Shasta as a "girly-girl" who liked to wear her hair long and paint her nails. She also liked to play with dolls, as any girl her age would. Dylan liked sports and playing outside.

Mark McKenzie was described as an outdoors enthusiast who liked to spend his spare time hunting and fishing. He worked full-time, making the bulk of the living for the family, as a supervisor at a stainless steel sink manufacturing company in Spokane, Washington, located just across Idaho's western border. Both Mark and Brenda were known to associate with bikers whose visits to their home sometimes gave way to partying. Both appeared to be well-liked throughout the community and no one whom the investigators interviewed could understand how they could meet such a violent, vicious end. On the surface, nothing appeared to have been stolen. What could have been the motive for such carnage? To steal the two young children in the middle of the night?

THERE WAS A SECOND STRUCTURE ON THE PROPERTY, A wooden shed that could have been used as a workshop, along with several vehicles in varying states of functionality, parked in the driveway or the yard, since there was no garage. The detectives wanted to have a look at all of them.

Parked in the bushes was a green Lincoln Continental that appeared to be a late 1970s model without a license plate. There was also a silver Chevrolet, a 4x4 extended cab pickup truck, on the front seat of which lay a rifle. The truck, the detectives learned, was registered to Mark McKenzie. Parked directly in front of the pickup was a silver-and-black Ford Bronco that, like the Lincoln, did not have any license plates. It had multiple bullet holes in it, as though it had been used for occasional target practice. Just west of the entrance to the property was a 1977 Starcraft motor home, white and tan, bearing Montana license plates, that, Maskell and Mattos were told, people lived in from time to time. Parked alongside it was a blue Dodge Ram pickup truck with Idaho license plates, and just south of the property was a red Chevrolet Blazer, also with Idaho plates.

The property adjacent to McKenzie's was owned by Robert Hollingsworth, the man who had first alerted the sheriff's department to the blood. Parked on

Hollingsworth's property was a silver-colored, 1988 Ford pickup truck with Idaho license plates, registered to Lisa and Daniel Miller. That vehicle, according to Hollingsworth, had shown up at the McKenzie home on Sunday, May 15, at approximately 8 P.M. It was the same vehicle that had unexpectedly turned up on Hollingsworth's property. Hollingsworth had discovered it at about 6:30 A.M. on Monday, May 16, when he had gone out to take care of his livestock. Hollingsworth had no idea why the truck had appeared on his property.

Detectives found a fresh roll of duct tape lying in the bed of the pickup, alongside a wadded-up ball of used duct tape, with grass clippings and other debris adhering to it. That truck, because it had been seen on the property where the crimes had occurred, and because duct tape had been used to bind the victims, suddenly took on greater significance. The truck, the detectives observed, could easily have been driven across a pasture area from McKenzie's property to Hollingsworth's without being seen, particularly at night.

On the evening of May 16, Maskell, accompanied by Prosecuting Attorney William Douglas and Deputy Prosecuting Attorney Donna Gardner appeared before Magistrate Judge Scott Wayman, and presented the first of many requests for warrants. In this instance the warrant applied for was for the vehicles on the property, as well as the vehicle on Hollingsworth's land. They were looking for blood, DNA, fibers, hairs, fingerprints and so forth. The judge granted the request.

—CHAPTER FOUR—

DETECTIVES MASKELL AND MATTOS, AS WELL AS SEVERAL other investigators with the Kootenai County Sheriff's Department, worked the investigation from two sides—one focused on the triple homicide, the other on finding the missing Shasta and Dylan Groene. In their efforts to find the children, the nearby countryside was searched thoroughly, particularly on the east side of Coeur d'Alene Lake, because that area was nearest the house. Helicopters conducted the search effort from the air and the Kootenai County Search and Rescue Council continued their efforts on the ground. The nationwide Amber Alert that had been issued by the Idaho State Police was quickly picked up by several Western states and in practically no time made its way to police agencies around the country. The alert also began showing up on websites, radio and television.

The children, however, were nowhere to be found.

News of Slade Groene's death found its way quickly to Lakes Middle School where he was in the seventh grade. The vicious manner of his death, as well as the death of his mother and her boyfriend, shocked the students and faculty. The school's principal, Chris Hammons, made it a point to visit all of the classrooms to talk about the terrible, sad events that had transpired.

"Many of the kids knew Slade, so they're grieving," Hammons told reporters.

Shasta and Dylan were students at Fernan Elementary School in Coeur d'Alene, where teachers and students were horrified. School personnel, including counselors, were available to any of the students who felt that they needed to talk about what had occured.

"Children are asking why it happened," said School District Superintendent Harry Amend. "This district is hurting right now. It's a very difficult, difficult time. This whole unknown business about the missing kids being gone puts a tough dynamic on it . . . Shasta and Dylan are two physically tiny, little bright-eyed kids— just very innocent bright-eyed kids."

Meanwhile, according to information released by the Kootenai County Sheriff's Department on Tuesday, May 17, a "person of interest" had surfaced in the case following interviews with relatives and friends of the victims. Robert Roy Lutner, 33, also known as "Concrete Bob," a moniker he had been given because of his work in the concrete and construction industry, was a friend of the victims and had visited them twice in recent days—once on the Friday afternoon preceding the murders and again on Sunday evening, perhaps only hours prior to the slayings. Brenda's son, Jesse Groene, told the detectives that Lutner owed Brenda Groene and Mark McKenzie $2,000. However, Jesse also told the investigators that none of his relatives had indicated that there might have been any trouble between Lutner and the victims, and there was no indication that he was being pressured to repay the money, even though the family needed it.

"I never saw him hostile toward my family at all," Jesse said.

No one in the family believed that Lutner had anything to do with the homicides.

Further investigation revealed that Lutner had been in trouble with the law before, and in fact, his criminal record in the county was somewhat lengthy. He had been in trouble on drug possession charges in 1992, and had been arrested for domestic battery in 2004 after a fight with his girlfriend outside a bar. That charge had been reduced to disturbing the peace. He'd been convicted twice for fraud in connection with improperly representing unemployment claims, for which he was currently on probation. Lutner was someone the cops definitely wanted to talk to. However, they first had to find the 6-foot-3-inch, 230-pound man.

He had been seen in an area bar on Sunday afternoon, prior to being at Groene and McKenzie's home on Frontage Road that day. Two days later, on Tuesday, he'd talked to his probation officer on the telephone and said that he was taking a trip to Boise. By that time, he had heard about the murders and was crying when he called a friend of the victims. Shortly after that, authorities began looking for him as a person of interest. According to the sheriff's department, Lutner was believed to have been driving either a 1975 Ford pickup, silver in color, with Idaho license plates, or a 1990 white Toyota pickup, also with Idaho plates.

Insisting that Lutner was only a "person of interest" and not a suspect in the murder investigation, Captain

Ben Wolfinger said that he would be "the first one out here dancing around if we had someone," indicating the degree of happiness he would be feeling for having a suspect.

Lutner's status did not last long. The next day, Wednesday, May 18, Lutner learned that the authorities were looking for him and he turned himself in to sheriff's deputies in Coeur d'Alene after returning from Boise. He was interviewed over the next several hours and denied having anything to do with the murders. He consented to take a polygraph examination and passed it with flying colors, and was subsequently dropped as a person of interest in the case, leaving Maskell and Mattos back at square one.

As the hours ticked away, there was still much activity in and around Mark McKenzie's home, which was cordoned off with yellow police tape. Investigators came and went from the tents that had been set up on the property's perimeter to help shield the crime sleuths from the rain as they searched for clues. The entire force from the FBI's Coeur d'Alene office, which was comprised of eight agents, joined in the effort to find Shasta and Dylan, along with the Idaho State Police, and investigators from the City of Spokane and Spokane County who volunteered their assistance.

"We'll probably be here for two or three days," Sheriff Rocky Watson said. According to Watson, the investigation was moving as quickly as possible because they were trying to find clues that would lead not only to the killer but, hopefully, to the missing children as well. "We're trying to do everything early because time is of the essence with the children."

—CHAPTER FIVE—

DEFINITIVE AUTOPSIES ON THE BODIES OF SLADE AND Brenda Groene and Mark McKenzie revealed that they had not been shot as originally suspected; all three had been bludgeoned to death, sustaining skull fractures and brain contusions, after being bound with duct tape and 18-inch plastic zip ties. Although the investigators were not yet saying publicly or officially what they believed the murder weapon may have been, the local newspaper reported that a claw hammer or some other blunt instrument had possibly been used.

A toxicology analysis would later reveal that traces of tetrahydrocannabinol, also known as THC, the active ingredient in marijuana, had been found in the blood of Brenda Groene and Mark McKenzie, along with traces of methamphetamine. Investigators claimed that they did not know the extent of the couple's drug use, whether it was merely recreational or more serious, and said that they still did not know whether the victims had been killed by one person acting alone or by more than one perpetrator. However, due to the fact that each victim had been bound, they theorized that it may have taken more than one person to carry out the crimes.

Wolfinger, along with Sheriff Rocky Watson, said

that investigators did not yet know whether the killer or killers had been acquainted with any of the victims. The fact that there was no forced entry to the house indicated that the victims may have opened their door to someone they knew. It also puzzled the detectives how, with all of the firearms found inside the house, the perpetrator had been able to subdue the victims without a fight. They theorized that the killer or killers might have used the element of surprise and sneaked up on them under cover of darkness, waiting until everyone had gone to bed, and parking a good distance from the house so that the sound of his car would not awaken anyone. Since there were no signs of forced entry, the detectives presumed that, just as the responding deputies had surmised, the killer had entered through the rear kitchen door, which had been left unlocked, as is common in communities where the crime rate is low and people have little reason to fear for their safety.

The detectives theorized that the killer or killers had entered the house well prepared, likely carrying a weapon with which to threaten the victims, along with the duct tape, zip ties and bludgeon. But who did he awaken first? Mark McKenzie and Brenda Groene? Or Slade? Did he bring them from their bedrooms and bind them one at a time while the others watched and did nothing? The fact that whoever had committed the murders was able to bind the victims without a struggle suggested that he'd either had assistance from others or was holding a firearm, or that perhaps he had held a gun on one of the adults and forced them to bind the others, leaving only one person for the perpetrator to bind.

How much of the carnage, if any, had Shasta and Dylan seen?

Questions and more questions ran through each investigator's mind as they tried to unravel the mystery of what had happened at the house on Frontage Road. The answers were slow in coming.

Before being cleared, "Concrete Bob" Lutner had confirmed that there'd had been a get-together at McKenzie's home on Sunday evening. Investigators had collected a number of fingerprints at the house.

"We need to talk to these folks and we need to get their elimination prints so that we can figure out who was there legitimately and who may be involved in this crime," Captain Ben Wolfinger said. Lutner had not been able to tell the detectives how many people had attended their party, but he did say that everyone who had resided in that house had been at home that evening, including Shasta and Dylan.

Were the children still alive? It was the big question on everyone's mind.

"I've got to believe they're alive, I need to believe that," Watson said. "I'm putting all of it on the fact or question of, Why would someone kill five people to throw two bodies inside a car and leave?"

During the first twelve hours of the investigation, two telephone lines at the sheriff's office were dedicated as "tip" lines, where people could call in anything at all regarding the case, from suspicions as to who might have committed the killings to information on the whereabouts of Shasta and Dylan. The calls were routed through the county's Emergency Operations Center, and volunteers set up shop with a bank of telephones in the basement of the sheriff's department. More than 150 calls had been received during that first twelve hours. There were up to six people on the phones at all times, each of whom had been trained to ask the right questions while collecting the information from the callers. They took the calls from concerned citizens, friends of the family, and an occasional psychic trying to be helpful with a thoughtful lead regarding Shasta and Dylan's whereabouts. Some of the tips came from parents whose children had known Shasta and Dylan and had told their parents about the outdoor locations where they had sometimes gone to play.

Searchers had found many of the areas described by the children, including play "forts" that they had built in the hills, and search dogs had picked up their scent at various locations in the hills or along the lakefront, as well as near ponds and streams that were searched with the aid of diving teams, to no avail. There simply was no sign of the children, and information was slow in developing.

"We don't know if they're injured," Captain Ben Wolfinger said. "We don't know if they're hiding out, if they're so scared they're afraid to come out. We want to search every nook and cranny."

Watson had assembled many of the searchers into teams in order to conduct grid searches in the vicinity of the house in the event that the children had run away to escape the same fate that had met the others, perhaps finding a hiding place, and dying there.

"Shasta and Dylan," Watson said, "know every rock, every crevice, and with that crime scene, we have no idea whether those kids are injured or not."

"We're looking for anything right now," Wolfinger added. "Whether it be the children themselves, the children's bodies or evidence, such as a scrap of clothing, anything like that."

Although there was much speculation circulating throughout the area about what the killer or killers' motive might have been, the possibility of a drug lab came up. Sheriff Watson, however, was quick to contradict that line of thinking.

"We've busted a lot of drug labs. [Residents of drug labs] don't mow their lawns and plant flowers, and she did," Watson said, referring to Brenda Groene. Watson added that the house was not a methamphetamine lab, and the investigators had not seen any evidence of drugs when they had processed it.

Gang involvement was also brought up, but was just as quickly dismissed by Watson. The Spokane County gang unit had examined the scene, and they failed to see any of the tell-tale signs. The crimes, he said, just didn't fit the patterns normally associated with gang activity.

Nonetheless, both Watson and Wolfinger agreed that because the case was so bizarre, anything was possible.

"We're not ruling anything out at this time," Wolfinger said. "There's no door closed on anything except Mr. Lutner," he added. Lutner had been completely cleared of crimes associated with the case.

A white trailer was parked near the crime scene and was used as a command post where detectives kept track of clues with computers, and organized evidence and search data.

Six investigators from the Idaho State Police assisted the seven investigators and numerous deputies from

Kootenai County, some of them processing the crime scene, others conducting interviews. Every area where blood was found was carefully examined and the evidence that was collected was sent off to the FBI in Virginia for a thorough DNA analysis.

"We keep processing the scene with the idea that maybe we'll get that one clue that will lead us to where the children are at or who they may be with," Wolfinger said.

As one day followed another, additional investigators from the FBI as well as from other local agencies joined in the investigation and the search. The FBI also offered $100,000 in reward money for information leading to the safe return of the children and the capture of the person or persons who had abducted them.

—CHAPTER SIX—

ON THE EVENING OF THURSDAY, MAY 19, 2005, MASKELL and Mattos received what may have been their first real break in the case. In Bonners Ferry, Idaho, about 75 miles north of Coeur d'Alene, near the Canadian and Montana borders, a white van with Washington license plates was seen at Roundheels Sports, a store that caters to hunters and fishermen. The shopkeeper called the Boundary County Sheriff's Office after a man and two children got out of the van and came into the store. The shopkeeper told deputies that the man had asked for directions to Libby, Montana, just across the border from Bonners Ferry, then left.

Sheriff's deputies and state troopers searched the main highway as well as the lesser-traveled roads between Bonners Ferry and Libby, but there was no sign of the van. It had either traveled beyond Libby by that time or had disappeared onto one of the many side roads in and around Bonners Ferry.

"Every tip that comes in is going to be investigated," said Coeur d'Alene Police Sergeant Christie Wood. "At this point, nothing has come of the Bonners Ferry tip."

• • •

ON THURSDAY, MAY 19, ON NATIONAL TELEVISION, Brenda's ex-husband and Shasta and Dylan's biological father, Steve Groene, 48, made an emotional plea for the safe return of his children.

"Please, please release my children safely," Groene said quietly, his voice hoarse from crying, as friends and relatives huddled around him. "They had nothing to do with any of this. Release them in a safe area where law enforcement can find them. Call the help line. Let them know where they can be found."

Groene did not take any questions from reporters afterward. Captain Ben Wolfinger apparently found Groene's statement interesting, particularly the reference that the children "had nothing to do with any of this." He would comment about it to reporters later.

"Is he emotional already?" Wolfinger asked aloud. "Yeah. Is he stressed? Yeah. Is he beside himself with grief? Yeah. However, there is no evidence to substantiate Steve Groene as a suspect or a person of interest." Wolfinger stopped short, however, of saying that Groene was off the hook. Victims' husbands are always looked at as possible suspects in any homicide investigation. Groene was later discounted as a suspect in both the murder and the kidnapping.

As news of the mysterious triple murder and the disappearance of Shasta and Dylan made its way across the nation, the public could not seem to get enough information about the case, despite the media efforts to report on it. There were numerous satellite television production vehicles at the somewhat remote location providing video and audio feed for such shows as *A Current Affair* and *Amer-*

ica's Most Wanted, as well as news agencies such as Fox News, MSNBC, and CNN. Court TV also did its share of reporting on the case, as did reporters for various newspapers and radio stations. The publicity helped the sheriff's department collect pledges of more than $70,000 in reward money to be distributed through a Secret Witness Program to people who provided information that turned out to be useful. It did not take long for the reward fund to reach $107,000.

Two days later, *America's Most Wanted* ran a segment on the investigation on its Saturday night telecast which resulted in nineteen tips to the sheriff's department. However, none of the tips provided much hope to the investigators that they would find the children anytime soon.

Sunday night, May 22, Geraldo Rivera was at the Kootenai County Fairgrounds with his show, *At Large*. Steve Groene appeared on the show, which was broadcast live, and told Rivera's national audience that the FBI believed he had not been truthful with them.

According to Groene, the FBI polygraph examiner told him: "Steve, I have to tell you, I have doubts. You haven't passed portions of this polygraph."

"Tell me the manner in which he told you," Rivera led him: "He was pretty gruff, wasn't he? Mimic him."

"He basically said, 'You know something about the whereabouts of your children,'" Groene replied. "'I think you need to tell us now.' Obviously, I said, 'No way,'" meaning that he did not know anything about the murders or his childrens' whereabouts.

Groene stated that he and Brenda had bickered prior to the killings. Groene said that he had asked Brenda for permission to have the children for an unscheduled visit.

He said that he only wanted them for a few days prior to a two-week vacation. Their disagreement had occurred on Friday, May 13, and Brenda had refused to allow his request.

Groene told Rivera and his viewers that he resided in the same house as Brenda's mother, but that neither she nor anyone else saw him come home on Sunday, May 15. Groene could not substantiate an alibi from about 10 P.M. Sunday until approximately 6 A.M. Monday, the approximate time of the killings. His former mother-in-law did not see him come home, and no one else saw him until he went to work on Monday morning.

The use of illicit drugs came up during the interview. Groene said that although he and Brenda had argued in the past over his belief that she and McKenzie were using methamphetamine, he had only heard rumors that they were using drugs and had no proof of it. He said that, assuming the rumors were true, he had been concerned that they might be using the drugs in front of the children. His own prior drug use also came up during the investigation, and he told Rivera that he had been forthright with investigators about his drug history following DNA and urine testing.

"I was truthful with them about any alcohol use, my drug history," Steve Groene said. "I had a pretty heavy drug history when I was younger. I did not lie."

Vance Groene, an older brother of Slade, Shasta, Dylan and Jesse, told Rivera that he had moved out of the McKenzie home because of increased tension, in part, he said, over drug usage in the past year.

"I knew their use to be recreational," Vance Groene said. "It was pretty easy to tell when my mom was high and when she wasn't." Vance said that he believed his mother, Slade and McKenzie were killed by people they knew. He said that the family dogs were not friendly to strangers, and would not allow anyone they didn't recognize close to the house without barking. The dogs were even known to bark at the neighbors. "It leads me to believe it was somebody who was welcomed into the home," he said.

Steve Groene's brother-in-law, Bob Price, told *Coeur d'Alene Press* reporter Dave Turner that Jesse Groene had also been accused of withholding information during his polygraph examination.

"Jesse informed Steve that he failed the test over a question about knowing the whereabouts of Dylan and Shasta," Price told Turner. "They [investigators] were slamming their fingers on the table and claiming he did know. He didn't know. We learned this shortly after Jesse's test."

Price told the reporter that he believed Steve Groene was not involved in the killings or the abductions.

"We can only imagine the kind of grief he's going through," Price said.

Steve Groene believed that the tremendous publicity that the case received caused the public to believe that he had something to do with the murders and the disappearance.

"There's people out there who still think I had something to do with this," Groene said. "All I can say is— get a life. Try to worry about yours."

Steve Groene said that he would be willing to take another polygraph, under one condition—that several others whose names he would provide to the investigators would take the test, too.

"I would have a list of about thirty names that they would have to prove to me have taken their test first before I take a second one," Groene said. "I would think that I'm as much a suspect as any other family member or any acquaintance or any friends that they had."

Like his son, Steve Groene thought that the victims had known their killer.

"Do I think it was one of their friends?" he asked. "Yeah." However, he admitted that he did not know many of Brenda's or Mark's friends. "My involvement with Mark and Brenda was calling to get my kids, and that was it. Otherwise, I really tried hard not to have contact with them."

In addition to the efforts that the various police agencies were making, Steve Groene opened up his own tip line and offered his $25,000 motorcycle as a reward for anyone who came forward with useful information. Although he began receiving a number of calls, none of them had any value.

"I get calls from reporters, from people who want to know if I've contacted psychics," Groene said. "I have had calls from people asking me to follow up and see if the detectives are looking into things they called in on the tip line already."

Sheriff Rocky Watson insisted that nobody had been eliminated yet as a suspect, but he was quick to discount that Steven Groene or any other member of his family was under serious suspicion.

What did the sheriff have to say about all of the prattle over the lie detector tests?

"We've done many polygraphs in this case," Watson said. "We don't comment about any of them."

—CHAPTER SEVEN—

By TUESDAY, MAY 24, THIRTY ADDITIONAL INVESTIGATORS from the FBI joined the massive effort already underway. The added manpower included agents specializing in kidnapping cases, and additional technicians to process the massive amount of evidence that had been collected. They brought along a team of profilers from Quantico, Virginia, who began developing a psychological profile of the killer or killers based on everything that was found at the crime scene and the nature of the crimes themselves. This raised the total number of people working the case to approximately 150. Joining them were a number of volunteers who had been working on the case from its outset.

"When we did the ground search the other day," Captain Ben Wolfinger said, "we had two hundred trained professional searchers come out. People just want to come and help in this case. It's been pretty incredible, and it's an ever-expanding thing." Wolfinger told reporters that more than 900 calls had been received on the tip line.

Special Agent Timothy J. Fuhrman, during a joint press conference with Kootenai County Sheriff Rocky Watson, publicized the $100,000 reward money that the

FBI had offered for information about the case or the location of the two children.

"This is just another tool in our bag to generate that information and give us what we hope is a happy resolution," Fuhrman told reporters.

According to Wolfinger, the investigators had the identities of the people who attended the party at the McKenzie home on Sunday, May 15, and they had contacted and interviewed all of them. None of those people, he said, had been singled out as a suspect or as a person of interest, and it did not appear likely that anyone from the list of party attendees would be. Wolfinger stated at the news conference that investigators were also satisfied that Steve Groene was not a suspect, nor was any other member of his family.

Those who knew Groene went even further by stating that he was totally innocent of the murders and abductions.

"He would never do that," said a close friend of Brenda Groene's. "He's a basket case right now. I think he's thinking the worst right now [with regard to the children]. A lot of us are."

The friend described Brenda Groene and Mark McKenzie as tough "hillbilly folks and proud of it," and speculated that it would have taken more than one person to overpower the couple.

"This is a senseless tragedy as far as I can tell," the friend said. "But you know . . . one minute I think I've got it figured out in my head, and the next minute I think it could be something else . . . My life has changed. I'm never going to live it the same." The friend resided in a rural area with few neighbors and now became edgy when a strange car passed by her house. She also kept her doors and windows locked, a practice that she hadn't even thought about prior to the murders.

On Tuesday night, the eve of memorial services for Brenda and Slade, at least 150 people gathered at the Kootenai County Fairgrounds in Coeur d'Alene to pray for the murder victims and for the safe return of Shasta and Dylan. The candlelight vigil drew relatives of the victims as well as people from all over the community.

"It's just to pray," said Wendy Price, an aunt of Slade, Shasta and Dylan. "If they see this, hopefully it will soften somebody's heart."

Steve Groene was also in attendance, as were at least two pastors from area churches who led the group in prayer.

"Would you bless the families tonight as they go to sleeplessness?" said one of the ministers as he prayed holding a candle while standing in the middle of the field. "I tell you, we've been with some heartbroken people."

"God, we know you love little children," said another preacher. "We know that you can move mountains. Lord, we know you can bring these kids back and we just ask that right now."

As the candles flickered in the night breeze, Shasta and Dylan's photographs could be seen hanging from a small shrine of sorts that someone had erected. There were several moments of silence during the vigil, and people could be heard weeping as they clung to each other in tears, their only hope being that Shasta and Dylan would turn up alive.

—CHAPTER EIGHT—

MARK MCKENZIE WAS CHARACTERIZED BY THOSE WHO knew him as a caring and hard-working man, who treated Brenda Groene's children as if they were his own. He would take them out to local streams to catch crayfish—also known as "crawdads"—and he often took Slade out into the woods to teach him how to track deer and elk. He was also portrayed as a man who always got up and went to work at his job. He was a manager at Spokane Stainless Products, a position that he had worked his way up to after initially being hired as a commercial sink installer. It was typical for him to start his day at 5 A.M., and he normally would not return home until 5 P.M. or later, easily working ten-hour days, with additional hours driving between Coeur d'Alene and Spokane. He had worked at the job for more than fifteen years, and barely missed a day. He had no known criminal record.

"His job was pretty hard," said his brother, Steve McKenzie. "His boss was pretty demanding. The idea of him being under the influence, being strung out, certainly would not have gone unnoticed . . . It's the only job I remember him having . . . Mark and Brenda were good people. The media has pounded on the rampant drug use out there. It wasn't true. . . . Yeah, they drank beer, and they smoked pot."

McKenzie said that the media had blown their partying out of proportion. There were never any problems, and he said that he always felt comfortable leaving his son there to play with Brenda's kids. He said that had things been otherwise, like what was being reported in the media, he wouldn't have even gone out to their house to visit or to leave his son there.

Steve McKenzie said that he last saw his brother on Sunday, May 15, when he stopped by Mark's home to drop off his son to play with Shasta and Dylan while he went to visit his and Mark's father, Ralph McKenzie. He said that he returned a few hours later and everything seemed normal.

"Nothing was out of the ordinary," McKenzie said. "Mark was unloading firewood. He didn't mention anything about any conflicts with anybody, or have any reason to be nervous about anything. They weren't drinking. In fact, they were talking about going out to rent some movies."

McKenzie told detectives that his brother and Brenda had some friends that he considered the responsible type, and others who liked to party. Brenda and his brother simply associated with both types of people.

"Some of their friends were your normal people that get up, go to work, and do the best that they can," he said. "There were also people who went out to their home just to drink beer and do the party thing."

Ken Francis, a friend who had known Mark for more than twenty years, characterized him as someone who

liked to hunt bear, cougar, deer and elk, and who generally liked to spend as much time outdoors as possible.

"He wasn't happy unless he was outside all the time,"
Francis said. "If I was in the area, I always stopped by to
see him. I knew he was there. Now he's not there anymore, and it's hard."

Francis also stopped by on Sunday, May 15, but he
said that he did not notice anything unusual. He also did
not leave McKenzie's home with the impression that a
party had been planned for that evening.

When preliminary results of blood evidence collected
at the crime scene came back from the FBI's forensic
laboratory, investigators, as well as family members,
were somewhat relieved when they learned that none of
the samples tested turned up any of Shasta or Dylan's
DNA. All of the blood that had been tested up to that
point belonged to Brenda, Slade and Mark. The news
provided new hope that the children were still alive
somewhere. But where?

"We still believe the children are alive," Wolfinger
stated during the daily news conference. "We always
had that assumption, but this news just bolsters that."

"It's good news after two weeks of bad news," Steve
McKenzie told reporters.

On Thursday, May 26, because the children were still
missing and a suspect had not been identified, the effort
to find clues relating to the triple murder and the abductions of Shasta and Dylan intensified and moved to the
Kootenai County Landfill. In response to reporters'
questions, Wolfinger emphasized that they were looking
for clues that might lead to a suspect, not bodies. He
said that investigators were searching for evidence such

as a potential murder weapon. It could be a tool or other instrument, he said, but stopped short of being specific as to what investigators believe may have been used to kill the victims. They were also looking for bloody clothing that might have been discarded by the killer before he fled the area, or anything else that might prove relevant to the case. Wolfinger said that his people, as well as FBI evidence technicians, would spend between five and ten days sifting through approximately forty tons of garbage that had been collected from the Wolf Creek area.

According to Sheriff Rocky Watson, there had been only two child abduction cases from Kootenai County in recent history that were not custodial-related. In 1980 Jodie Aldrich, 4 years old, was abducted from a daycare center in Hayden, but was, fortunately, found alive a few days later in a land pit in the vicinity of U.S. Highway 95 and Idaho Highway 53. In the second case, 2-year-old Ryan Hoeffliger disappeared from his home in November 1984. The toddler was found dead several hours later, his body floating beneath a private boat dock less than two miles from his home. Watson believes that the Aldrich child was released because of the intense media coverage; her abductor may have realized that the public attention focused on her case might lead to his discovery and arrest if he kept her. Watson was hoping that a similar scenario would play out with Shasta and Dylan because of the extensive news coverage surrounding them.

"I want the guy to pull into a rest area and toss the kids out," Watson told reporters.

—CHAPTER NINE—

ON FRIDAY, MAY 27, TOURISTS BEGAN ARRIVING AT THE Wolf Lodge Campground, located near the house that Brenda Groene and Mark McKenzie had shared along the shores of Coeur d'Alene Lake. It was Memorial Day weekend and the temperature had remained unseasonably warm, registering in the 80s. The campground, which featured rustic cabins and a creek, catered to families, and many had shown up early Friday trying to get a head start on the holiday crowds. Most families were not afraid to come into the area because, they reasoned, the media spotlight on the senseless tragedy had likely made the killer or killers move on to another location. However, despite the coming and going of the tourists, an eerie stillness permeated the area that weekend. The campground, nonetheless, hadn't suffered much as far as business was concerned, according to manager Susan Harrison.

"We only lost a few customers, and those were with children. It just kind of went back to everyday business."

Harrison and her husband, both retired, had arrived with their RV at the campground in their capacity as hosts/managers only a few days before the killings and abductions had occurred. Although they had made the best of being in the midst of the tragedy and the resulting investigation, they couldn't help but reflect on the circumstances.

"I never in my wildest imagination thought that coming to Coeur d'Alene Lake would put me in the middle of a triple homicide," Susan Harrison said. "We're keeping our eyes open. We're always checking, but we have a sense they're not around here," she added.

One camper, traveling with a group of sixteen, had come from Montana, where the case had received considerable media attention, but no one had considered, even for a moment, canceling their plans.

"We didn't realize it was this close," said the camper. "Still, what can you say?"

"I had no idea that we were right next to it," said another camper. "But Coeur d'Alene is so spread out. You hear these things, but do you think, 'Oh my gosh! I'm changing my plans to go to Coeur d'Alene'? These things happen everywhere you go."

"I think my daughter said it will probably be the safest place to camp because of all of the police," said yet another camper.

By THE FOLLOWING AFTERNOON, CAPTAIN BEN WOLFINGer held another press conference in which he asked campers and others enjoying the forests that weekend to keep an eye out for anything unusual, particularly anything that might turn out to be a potential clue. He also asked tourists to look for Shasta and Dylan at the highway rest stops, as well as at restaurants and gas stations.

Although Wolfinger said that the investigators were still searching the landfill and analyzing evidence, they had not received any new leads to bring them any closer to clearing the case or finding the children. He had nothing but praise for the investigators who put in long days at the landfill, wearing hot protective clothing, only to come home long enough to clean up and perhaps eat and then return to the command post at the crime scene to continue analyzing evidence.

"It's nice to know that's the kind of dedication we have in the whole incident, working this case," Wolfinger said.

While the investigators from the various agencies continued their work, the National Center for Missing and Exploited Children had issued posters with photos of Shasta and Dylan, as well as updated information about them, which they began distributing in lots of 10,000 by faxing them to businesses, particularly hotels and restaurants throughout the western U.S. and western Canada. That same evening, *America's Most Wanted* was planning to dedicate another segment of their show to the missing children in the hope that it would result in leads to their whereabouts.

"Every day we're looking for that one phone call, the one piece of evidence and that one tip that will bring us closer to finding the children," Wolfinger said. "But we don't have that yet."

SOME SIX WEEKS EARLIER, PRIOR TO THE WOLF LODGE tragedy and the abductions of Shasta and Dylan, Sheriff Rocky Watson had written a letter to Idaho Governor Dirk Kempthorne addressing his concerns regarding Idaho's relatively new "Amber Alert" system, which had replaced the statewide system that had been in operation for the past eight years. In his letter, Watson had stated that the manner in which the current system was set up could cause delays in getting the word out about missing children, particularly in the northern part of the state. He was frustrated, and his concerns were brought to light when Shasta and Dylan disappeared. There were clearly delays in getting the word out about them.

Part of the delay was caused by the fact that the murders and abductions likely occurred either on Sunday night, May 15, or Monday morning, May 16—but the grisly discovery of the victims' bodies was not made until that Monday evening and it wasn't until late in the evening of May 16 that investigators learned that there *might* be two children missing from the residence. In the early morning hours of May 17 they were reasonably certain that Shasta and Dylan were in fact missing. As a result, the Amber Alert did not get sent out until 4:30 A.M. on May 17.

After the Amber Alert was issued at 4:30 A.M., there were additional delays that were caused by the manner in which the state's system was set up. Protocol had to be followed, and although the original Amber Alert had been approved and issued at 4:30 A.M., the state's automatic system, in which the alert would have gone out to Idaho's communications center to be transmitted to various state agencies such as the Idaho Department of Transportation, the Idaho Lottery Commission, and local area broadcasters, did not get activated until 6:30 A.M. Upon activation, it would also show up on major highway electronic readerboards for passing motorists to read. Watson's argument was that it would have been more effective in getting the word out about the missing children if he had been allowed to activate the state's Emergency Alert System, a radio transmission network that is used to notify communities of an emergency. Local jurisdictions such as Watson's, however, do not have the authority to activate that particular system. If they had Watson would have immediately been able to notify authorities in Spokane to the west, and locales in Montana to the east.

The failure to get the word out promptly was a prime example of an ineffective bureaucracy at work. Someone did not activate the system at 6:30 A.M. because they questioned whether the information being provided met the criteria needed for the issuance of an Amber Alert. To make matters even worse, someone farther down the line at the state level questioned, again, whether the information met the criteria of an Amber Alert. By the time it was decided that the information did in fact meet the criteria, it was 8 A.M. before the information was released to broadcasters.

The Idaho Lottery Commission did not release the information about Shasta and Dylan to its customers until late in the afternoon that day, and readerboards in the area did not begin showing the information until approximately ten hours after the information's release, which would have been about 4 P.M. Neither Washington nor Montana activated their Amber Alert systems for Shasta and Dylan because their bureaucrats felt like the information did not meet the criteria. The reasons given for those states' failure to issue the Amber Alert, and also for the delays that occurred initially and throughout the day, were that the local sheriff's department did not know with 100 percent certainty that Shasta and Dylan had been abducted, they did not know how long the children had been missing and they did not have a description of a suspect's vehicle or a direction of travel.

"Eventually, the information is sent to broadcasters in Spokane for airing to the public," read a portion of Watson's letter to the governor. "This time delay is unacceptable when we must consider that it only takes minutes to be in another state or even into Canada for a fleeing abductor."

Statistics show that 74 percent of kidnapped children who end up being murdered are killed within three hours of the kidnapping. So what excuses were made to answer to the calls of incompetence regarding the Shasta and Dylan situation?

"We tripped up on this one," said Bill Bishop, Idaho's director of Homeland Security.

"Amber coordinators across the country and law enforcement using the Amber Alert are put in a balancing act," said Bob Hoever, a spokesperson for the National Center for Missing and Exploited Children. "They need to protect the safety and health of children, versus overusing the Amber Alert system and desensitizing the public."

Sheriff Watson, however, was told by Idaho Amber Alert director Vickie Miller that the state's Emergency Alert System could be activated only on the state's authority. It could not be activated by a local sheriff.

"Our system broke down when we used it," said Shoshone County Sheriff Chuck Reynolds, who also serves as president of the Idaho Sheriffs' Association. "The kids are what are important. To hell with the protocol sometimes. Let's get the information out there."

"They ignored us until there was a problem," Watson said. "Why does it have to fall apart first to get their attention?"

While the governor's office has agreed to look into the matter, the Idaho director of Homeland Security agrees that there is a problem and has also agreed to allow Sheriff Watson to issue alerts through the Emergency Alert System when necessary.

"We're not taking the Emergency Alert System away from Rocky," said Bill Bishop. "He's got a long and professional career. I think we can trust him."

—CHAPTER TEN—

THREE WEEKS INTO THE INVESTIGATION, DETECTIVES Maskell and Mattos weren't any closer to finding out who'd killed Brenda and Slade Groene and Mark McKenzie, and abducted Shasta and Dylan. There were leads from time to time, but nothing solid enough for the cops to go public with, much less give them much hope that they were getting close to solving the case. Although more than 700 interviews had been conducted and more than 1,700 tips had been called in, neither of the cops said much—they couldn't, and preserve the integrity of the investigation. There were things that only the cops and the murderer knew about the case, and it was important that it remained that way.

"It's a long way from a cold case or a dead end," said Sheriff Rocky Watson. "Every day there can't be breaking news. This is what makes investigators and investigations, when they keep the enthusiasm on the boring, tedious portions of it . . . There's always something to keep enthusiasm or motivation going. They've got leads following all traditional paths and there's a lot of leads."

Watson, being cautious in his statements, said that it was his opinion that the killings had been premeditated because whoever was responsible had brought the materials needed to bind the victims to the scene, as well as the device that was used to commit the murders.

"It was a highly emotional crime scene, a violent crime scene," Watson told reporters. "Real violent crimes are usually driven by love, money, or drugs . . . This is what I would expect from a Colombian drug lord sending a message to a dealer. But these people didn't have big drug or money issues."

The investigation had focused on those very issues at one time or another. They had looked at the love angle and found nothing. They had looked at the money angle, and even though they had learned that "Concrete Bob" Lutner had owed Brenda and Mark money, they had completely cleared him of having any involvement in the crimes. The fact that both Brenda and Mark had traces of marijuana and methamphetamine in their blood at the time of death was looked at carefully from several different angles, but again the only thing the investigators had determined was that both Brenda and Mark were recreational drug users. There didn't appear to be anything in their backgrounds that would have led to such senseless violence and the abduction of the two children.

Meanwhile Shasta and Dylan's family, as well as much of the community, had not given up hope that the children would turn up alive. The faculty and staff at Fernan Elementary School, which the two children had attended, had already begun making plans for their return in the fall, even though the start of the new school year was nearly three months away.

"We've been making up class lists," said Principal Lana Hamilton. "I've put Shasta and Dylan on class lists for the fall. We knew that we needed to think they were coming back."

Students, as well as staff members, also planted three flowering plum trees on the school's grounds for Shasta, Dylan and their slain brother Slade, even though he had gone to another school.

"We're there to support the Groene family and each other as we struggle through this difficult time," Hamilton said.

Shasta, a second-grader, had written a poem about her father, Steve Groene, before she disappeared. Her teacher presented it to her father during a school gathering that included students, faculty and other members of the Groene family. It was a heartfelt occasion that seemed to renew everyone's hope that the children would turn up alive.

"Steve and everyone on the Groene side of the family is still holding out all hopes," said Bob Price, Shasta and Dylan's uncle. "We're pleased that tips are still coming in . . . We know that the very best are on it. Nothing we can do is going to bring back Mark, Brenda or Slade, but how much time do the other children have left?"

IT WASN'T LONG BEFORE FATHER'S DAY CAME, AND STEVE Groene found that all he could do was wait for news of some sort about his missing kids, while hoping that they turned up alive. It was his Father's Day wish that they would be found safe and sound, but he had already prepared himself for the worst.

"I was pretty confident the first couple of weeks that we were going to find these kids, and that they were going to be okay," Groene told reporters. "Then the next couple of weeks, every day that they weren't found, it kind of hit that there's the possibility that they may never be found . . . Pretty much all I do is sit and wait for that phone call."

Groene had taken a leave of absence from his job at a Spokane, Washington, recycling center so that he could try to make some sense of what had occurred. He also stopped playing, at least temporarily, in a weekend blues band he had formed called Blue Tattoo.

Groene recalled the last time that he had seen Shasta, Dylan and Slade. It had been about three weeks prior to the murders, and the three kids had spent the weekend with him. He said that Dylan and Slade liked to play games on their PlayStation 2, and that Shasta liked to watch television with him.

"Shasta would cuddle on the couch with me and we'd watch TV," Groene said. It was too late for Slade, but Groene said that he misses all three of the children.

"I need Shasta and Dylan, and they need me," he said.

O N TUESDAY, JUNE 28, JESSE GROENE, 18, APPEARED BE-fore Judge John Mitchell for his sentencing hearing, which resulted as part of a plea agreement he had entered into on charges of burglary and grand theft. He had been caught shoplifting at a Post Falls, Idaho, Wal-Mart, and had been found in possession of a stolen Jeep on February 9, 2005. He had previously told police officers in Post Falls that he had been under the influence of marijuana and methamphetamine for five days before his arrest. While incarcerated, he had also been charged with kicking a jail door and damaging the lock mechanism. As part of his agreement, in which he agreed to plead guilty to the burglary and to damaging the jail door, the grand theft charge was dismissed. During his sentencing hearing he told the judge that he wanted to go straight after what had happened to his family, in part because of the fact that he believed that drugs might possibly have been involved.

"I don't know if I'm right for sure," Jesse Groene told the judge, "but I think it might have something to do with drugs. I found out in the worst way how drugs have ruined someone's life. Please let me prove to my family and myself that I have learned from this experience."

Noting that Jesse had the letters "NFP" tattooed on the back of his neck, the judge asked him what it meant and whether he had been to a tattoo parlor while out of jail on a furlough to attend his family members' funeral services.

"That was on my neck when I went to jail," he told the judge. He explained that the letters stand for "North Francis Pimps," a group of which he was a member.

"A lot of people think it's a gang, but really it's not," Jesse told the judge. "It's just a group of friends who are there for each other. It's nothing near a gang."

He explained that the "North Francis Pimps" do not wear gang colors, nor do they engage in drive-by shootings.

Could they have somehow been involved in the killings? People naturally wanted to know, and the judge indicated that he would be looking into the matter further.

Mitchell then sentenced Jesse Groene to 2 years in the state penitentiary, with a stipulation that he would retain jurisdiction over the matter under the condition that

Groene attend a six-month rehabilitation program at a state facility in Cottonwood, Idaho, operated by the Department of Corrections. He would be given probation after successfully completing the program; failing to do so would send him off to prison to serve out the complete term.

In the meantime, the investigation uncovered no evidence implicating the "North Francis Pimps" in any of the crimes that were committed at the McKenzie house on Frontage Road.

—CHAPTER ELEVEN—

As the days turned into weeks, and weeks into months, it began to seem more and more as if Shasta and Dylan had permanently disappeared. Then, on Saturday, July 2, at about 1:30 A.M., forty-eight days after the case had begun, the unexpected happened. A man fast approaching middle age, driving a red Jeep Cherokee with Missouri license plates, turned in to the parking lot of the Coeur d'Alene Denny's restaurant, located north of Interstate 90, and parked. He hurriedly exited the vehicle, accompanied by a little girl with an angry expression on her face. They walked briskly into the twenty-four-hour establishment, passing by two young men, Nick Chapman, 21, and Chris Donlan, 18, who were standing outside smoking cigarettes. Both would recall later that there was something strange about the man, but they didn't know what it was—whether it was just his demeanor or something about the way he looked.

Nick Chapman glanced at the man and the girl as they walked past, and then did a double take. In a near state of shock, he briefly made eye contact with the little girl. He recognized her as Shasta Groene. He had no doubt, he would later tell the police, that this was Shasta—he had seen a billboard with a photo of her and her brother, Dylan, earlier that evening.

But where was Dylan? Chapman wondered. There was no sign of him, yet he knew from all of the publicity the case had received that Dylan was missing, too, and should have been with his sister.

As the man and the girl entered the restaurant, there was a photo of Shasta posted in the foyer. The man glanced around to make sure that no one was looking at him; moments later, the photo had disappeared. After being seated, the man placed a food and drink order for himself and the little girl.

Chapman and Donlan remained outside for the moment as each thought about what they should do next. Chapman made sure that he wrote down the Jeep's license plate number, and convinced himself that he would not allow the man to leave the restaurant with Shasta. At the same time, Donlan alerted his girlfriend, Tessa Syth, 17, who was inside with Chapman's girlfriend, Raela Rhodes, 20, by sending her a text message on his cellular telephone. He told her what he had just seen.

"Teddy bear, that little girl looks line [sic] that Shasta girl," read a portion of the 1:42 A.M. text message.

Shasta and the man were sitting near the rear of the restaurant, about six booths away from Raela and Tessa. After he was certain that Tessa understood the message, Donlan and Chapman alerted Denny's employees about what they had seen as well.

A waitress, Amber Deahn, 25, had already recognized Shasta by that time, and had told her shift manager. The manager, noting that the time was 1:51 A.M., subsequently called 911. Four minutes later, Chapman also called 911 and reported what he and Donlan had witnessed. Nervous that they might do something to alert the man that they had recognized Shasta, Chapman and Donlan tried to remain calm as they re-entered the restaurant and took their seats at the booth with their girlfriends. Chapman took the copy of *Nickel's Worth*, a weekly classified ad newspaper, that Tessa had been reading. It had a copy of a poster of Shasta and Dylan inside it. With the page opened to the poster, he handed it to one of the waitresses. She acknowledged that she was aware of the situation.

"The restaurant was pretty much empty," Amber Deahn would later tell the police. "It was the calm before the storm." She explained that it was the quiet time prior to the bars closing, after which business would become brisk again for a while.

After briefly discussing how to handle the situation with the manager, Deahn went over to the table to try to give Shasta some crayons.

"I knew how the kids looked from the poster," Deahn said. "She was closed off, not a normal child. When you put crayons and masks in front of them, they usually light up. She just said, 'Thank you,' and looked at the man."

Approximately ten minutes later three police cars, one at a time, pulled into the restaurant's parking lot, their lights turned off. When the first police car arrived, the man with the girl motioned for the waitress to bring him his bill. He then got up, taking the little girl with him, and headed toward the restrooms. Watching him nervously, restaurant personnel reasoned that he must have seen the car through the windows when it turned in to the parking lot.

Did the man know that the cops were there because of him and Shasta? Or had he merely thought that they were stopping by for some late-night coffee, and just gotten up from his table with the girl in the hope that he could slip out undetected after the police officers had been seated?

Whatever the case, when the man returned a few minutes later, several officers approached him. Before the cops could escort him outside, the man leaned over the table and said something to the girl. If anyone heard what he had said to her, it was not revealed. It could have been a threat for her to keep her mouth shut, he could simply have told her good-bye or he could have said any number of other things.

"Hi, sweetie," Amber Deahn said to the girl while the police escorted the man outside. "What's your name, honey?"

"Shasta Groene," replied the little girl, who started crying.

Deahn picked Shasta up and held her in her arms and hugged her, trying to comfort her as best she could.

Shasta repeated to one of the officers, in response to his questions, that her name was Shasta Groene.

"I want my daddy," she cried. "I want to go home."

The as yet unidentified man complied with the police officers' requests as they instructed him to get into one of their patrol cars. He was then taken to the local jail.

Shasta, who appeared to be in good physical health, was taken to a nearby hospital for examination and observation, where she remained for the next couple of days. She was kept under close police supervision until she could be reunited with her father, who had to travel from Seattle to Coeur d'Alene to be with her.

"This just makes me happy," Chapman later told reporters of his experience of being a part of Shasta's rescue. "It's the most amazing, unreal, euphoric thing that could happen."

"It's like cramming all of the holidays together into one," agreed Donlan.

Meanwhile, everyone wondered what had happened to Dylan.

—CHAPTER TWELVE—

B Y SUNDAY, JULY 3, SHORTLY AFTER HIS ARREST, THE MAN with Shasta was positively identified as Joseph Edward Duncan III, a 42-year-old fugitive sex offender from Fargo, North Dakota. Upon request by the arresting officers, Duncan had produced a North Dakota driver's license. He would initially be charged with two counts of first-degree kidnapping, for which the maximum penalty in Idaho is life in prison or death. Those charges would be but the first of many as the detectives built their case against him. As his background was exposed little by little, the local populace would be shocked to learn that such a monster had been in their midst.

"It's a relief to find her," said Sheriff Rocky Watson. "We have had so many false sightings that there was a lot of disbelief on my part. I wasn't comfortable until I saw her at the hospital myself."

Family members, needless to say, were overjoyed with the news of Shasta's rescue. "I wasn't expecting anything less," Vance Groene said. Although he was ecstatic that his sister had been found, he expressed concerns about the whereabouts of his brother, Dylan.

Shasta's father, Steve, was in the Seattle area visiting his sister when he received the news of his daughter's rescue. His nephew immediately drove him back to Coeur d'Alene so that he could be reunited with Shasta.

Shasta was interviewed by Detectives Maskell and Mattos while she was still a patient at Kootenai Medical Center in Coeur d'Alene. Following the initial interviews, according to Captain Ben Wolfinger, it was not yet clear to detectives precisely where she had been for the past six weeks. Detectives had not yet questioned her about the events at her home the night the slayings occurred. They naturally wanted to take it easy with her and, since they had a suspect in custody, there was really no hurry now to get all of the intricate details. They decided instead that their focus of inquiry would be centered on what had become of Dylan, and to take things one step at a time. Wolfinger also said that it was not yet clear what role Duncan may have played in the entire scheme of things.

"He's certainly going to be looked at in that package of this heinous combination of crimes," Wolfinger said.

Maskell and Mattos immediately set about obtaining a search warrant for the red Jeep Cherokee that Duncan had been driving, which they now knew had been stolen in St. Paul, Minnesota, on May 4. According to Kootenai County Prosecutor Bill Douglas, other search warrants related to the case and Duncan's arrest were being processed.

"I'm really gratified that we've at least found Shasta," said Douglas. "But there's still a lot of unanswered questions and a long way to go."

"We'll go wherever the evidence leads," said Magistrate Judge Scott Wayman, who'd approved the initial search warrant.

"We're looking at a number of investigative leads to determine the situation involving Dylan," said FBI Special Agent in Charge Timothy J. Fuhrman. "Many times these cases are only solved through random sightings. There's no question the intense publicity contributed to the safe recovery of Shasta."

While the investigation continued in northern Idaho, officers in Fargo, North Dakota, were posted outside Duncan's apartment. They were there to guard it while investigators awaited the approval of a warrant to search his dwelling.

As THEY BEGAN BUILDING THEIR BACKGROUND ON DUNcan, detectives Maskell and Mattos learned that he was 42 years old at the time of his arrest, born February 25, 1963, and raised in Tacoma, Washington. His first run-in with the law occurred in 1978 when he was only 15 years old. In that incident he raped a 9-year-old boy at gunpoint, and the following year he was arrested driving a stolen car. He was sentenced as a juvenile and sent to Dyslin's boys' ranch in Tacoma, where he told a therapist who was assigned to his case that he had bound and sexually assaulted six boys. He also told the therapist that he estimated that he had raped thirteen younger boys by the time he was 16.

The detectives could only wonder about what he may have done to Shasta and Dylan over the past several weeks.

Two years later, in 1980, Duncan stole four handguns and ammunition from a neighbor's house in Tacoma, the detectives learned. Later that evening, he spotted a 14-year-old boy who had been walking alone in his neighborhood. Duncan abducted the boy, and raped him twice that night at gunpoint. Duncan was sentenced to 20 years in prison for those crimes.

Fourteen years later he was paroled on the condition that he have no contact with minor children, and was sent to a halfway house in Seattle. It did not appear that he was capable of going straight, however, and any hope of him returning to society as a normal, productive citizen quickly vanished. He violated his parole in 1996 by getting caught in possession of marijuana and for possession of a firearm. He was sent to jail for 30 days, and then released.

Maskell and Mattos learned that Duncan had relocated to Fargo, North Dakota, following his release from prison and had enrolled at North Dakota State University, where he was a computer science major. Although university officials would not discuss his student status, the detectives learned that he was enrolled as of the spring 2005 semester and that he was a senior expecting to graduate soon. He made the dean's list twice, and was a member of the Phi Kappa Phi honor society.

Upon his arrival in Fargo, Duncan had registered with the police department as a sex offender, as he was required to do, and he was classified as a Level III. Level III offenders are considered a high risk for recidivism. According to Fargo Police Captain Jeff Williams, Duncan had been following all the rules for sex offenders.

"As far as we know, he was more or less a model," Williams said.

Perhaps he was—until July 3, 2004, a year earlier,

when a felony complaint had been filed against him in Becker County District Court by the Detroit Lakes Police Department in the state of Minnesota. Detroit Lakes is located 45 miles east of Fargo, just across the border.

That fact brought forth chilling memories for Maskell and Mattos as they recalled how a man had been spotted in the border town of Bonners Ferry, Idaho, with two children who fit the descriptions of Shasta and Dylan, asking directions on how to get to Libby, Montana.

According to the complaint, the Detroit Lakes Police Department received a report of a sexual assault at a local middle school playground. When officers arrived at the scene to investigate, they met with two juvenile boys, ages 6 and 8. The boys told the officers that they had been playing there when a man drove up in a small shiny red car. The man, they said, walked to a secluded area near the playground equipment, and was carrying a video camera. He then called the boys over to where he was waiting. When they walked up to the man, he reached over and pulled down the shorts of the 6-year-old boy and touched his genitals. The man also attempted to pull down the shorts of the 8-year-old, but was unable to do so. The boys ran away, and the man left the area.

The 6-year-old boy was able to provide a physical description of the suspect. He said that the man had a noticeable "bump" on his top lip that touched his bottom lip when he spoke. Detroit Lakes Police Department investigator Chad Jutz entered the sketchy description that the boy provided into the Minnesota Bureau of Criminal Apprehension predatory data base. After the computer did its work, Jutz came up with a match: Joseph Edward Duncan III. The data also showed that Duncan drove a red two-door Pontiac Grand Am, and had a very pronounced bump on his upper lip.

Jutz put together a photo lineup of six male individuals, one of whom was Duncan, and showed it to the 6-year-old. After viewing the lineup for a few seconds, the boy picked Duncan from the group of photos and stated that this was the person who had touched his genitals at the middle school playground.

The cops also found another witness who told them that he had seen a red Pontiac Grand Am parked near the playground on the date of the assault.

Although the system had worked beautifully in showing that Duncan was the likely perpetrator of the Detroit Lakes assault, it had broken down somewhere along the way, because it took nine months—until March 4, 2005—for the complaint to actually get filed, and another month before Duncan was called in to face the charges before a judge.

Although Michael Fritz, the assistant prosecutor in Becker County, Minnesota, had asked for $25,000 bail at Duncan's arraignment there, the judge set his bail at $15,000 after Duncan's attorney, Dennis Fisher, argued that his client's bond be set at $10,000 so that "there is some opportunity for Mr. Duncan to preserve some of his resources." Fisher told the judge that Duncan was set to finish his degree in computer science within the month, and that he has some projects "he needs to address" to get his degree. Fisher explained that he worked as a software developer for a company in Fargo.

In setting Duncan's bail, the judge ordered that Duncan have no contact with his victims or other minors, that he not leave the area, that he agree to extradition in advance if it was needed, and that he report to his parole officer by telephone.

Almost immediately a local businessperson, Joe Crary, posted Duncan's $15,000 bond. Police would eventually learn that Duncan and Crary became acquainted while bicycling along Fargo bicycle trails. Duncan fled the state soon after posting bail with Crary's money.

—CHAPTER THIRTEEN—

NOTING THAT DUNCAN WAS "APPARENTLY QUITE A scholar," Detectives Brad Maskell and Dan Mattos discovered that Duncan had posted his résumé to an on-line job-finding service, claiming that he had held jobs in Spokane and Edmonds, Washington, and in Colorado during the 1990s. Most of the dates that he had listed on his résumé coincided with the time that he was in prison for the rape of the 14-year-old Tacoma boy. He stated that he liked karate, skiing and scuba diving, and said that he "hoped to relocate to a more southern state, possibly to the Kansas City region" when he finished his degree.

Maskell and Mattos also discovered that Duncan had created a blog, an online Web log, dedicated to opposing registration laws for sex offenders. Given his computer background, it wasn't surprising that Duncan had created such a site. He called it The Fifth Nail (http://fifthnail .blogspot.com), and posted to it frequently after its creation in January 2004. Many of the entries focused on Duncan's own sex crimes, and his obsession about the way in which sex offenders are treated by society. Surprisingly, he also sometimes wrote about his desire to get closer to God.

Duncan explained on the site why he called it "The Fifth Nail":

> According to myth gypsies crafted five nails for Christ's execution not four. The fifth nail was meant to pierce his heart, but the gypsies hid the fifth nail from the roman soldiers.

Duncan went on to write that the gypsies who made the nails were portrayed in mythical stories claiming that they were punished by God for causing Christ to suffer longer—in other stories that Duncan referred to, the gypsies were rewarded for trying to protect Christ. He also wrote that the "fifth nail" is supposedly a genuine sacred relic that has "miraculous" power.

The "mission statement" of Duncan's site stated that The Fifth Nail's purpose was to aid in the struggle opposing "official propaganda" that helps propagate intolerance toward certain "classes of people," i.e. sex offenders, who have been singled out because of prior mistakes or even those mistakes that they might make in the future.

Many of the entries, the detectives noted, provided some insight into the way Duncan's mind worked, particularly his thoughts in the days leading up to the Idaho killings and abductions. His first blog entry appears to have been written on January 4, 2004, in which he stated that he hoped that his website would serve as a "voice for oppressed 'criminals.'" He also stated that he wasn't being supportive of their criminal behavior but was supporting "the human being inside." He said that he was "trying to get people to see that punishing a scapegoat . . . only creates more victims, mostly innocent ones."

At one point he wrote about a sex crime that he'd committed when he "was very young," and described himself as a "kid acting out confusion over my own abuse." He claimed that he was not a pedophile, despite all of the evidence and convictions to the contrary. He said that when he was sentenced, he'd been sent to an adult sex offender program "where half the men in my 'treatment group' sat and fantasized about me."

He was also fond of posting song lyrics to the site, such as "Real, Real, Real" by Jesus Jones, "Losing My Religion" by R.E.M., and "Imagine" by John Lennon, which he believed was the "greatest song every [sic] written."

Some of the other entries that the detectives read were from January 4, 2004, through May 13, 2005. In one entry he stated that attacking criminal offenders would only cause society's problems to worsen, and that it was his hope that "society" would "wake up" and realize that "criminals are victims, too."

In another section of his blog, Duncan preached "love," and attempted to quote Jesus in the following passage: "What Jesus Really Said Was . . . 'I am the way, the truth, and the light. There is no other way to know the Father but by these (me).' "

He wrote of forgiveness for those who commit crimes, arguing that punishment "is just more crime" and that "the only cure for crime is Love." Christ teaches "love your enemy," he declared. "Not because God wants us to, but because our ultimate happiness depends upon it."

The foregoing passage gives one pause to wonder whether Duncan was really trying to say that we should love and forgive *him*, and others like him, of sexually abusing and even murdering our children and loved ones.

"If we had treated Germany with even a little respect," Duncan wrote in another entry, "(i.e. Love) after WWI, She would have never let Hitler lead her."

In an entry dated Monday, February 28, 2005, Duncan wrote that he is very knowledgeable about abuse. He claimed that he understands abuse from several perspectives, including the victims, offenders, and the abuse created by "the system." He claimed that he was not advocating that offenders should be allowed to do their "thing," and hinted that the authorities should take "direct measures" to prevent people from hurting one another. At one point he suggested that sex crimes could be substantially reduced by offering offenders free counseling, or even amnesty for offenders who agree to a treatment program.

"I doubt it will ever happen, though," Duncan wrote, "because our society loves the excitement that sex offenders bring into our living rooms through the media and we would be lost without someone to point our fingers at."

In another entry titled "What Friends Are For," he wrote about a female friend who warned him against dwelling on his sex-offender past and having such a negative approach to life:

> She is obviously correct, and it bothers me that I hadn't seen this before. Not that I'm really negative inside, I'm really not. I love my life, and I love the world, and I believe genuinely that God does not make mistakes, so there is nothing "wrong" about the way things are. I know from ongoing personal experience that my struggle to know the Truth is God(')s gift to me! . . . . . So, Thank you pretty neighbor

girl for pointing out this sad impression I've been giving and allowing me the opportunity to amend my ways.

As his blog entries moved into March and April, there was an obvious progression toward what appeared to be a more disturbing mindset. Duncan's ability to hang on to what society perceives as normalcy clearly began to deteriorate as he began to re-enter the multiple phases, or cycle, that a sex offender goes through, which will be explored in more detail later.

On April 1, he posted two entries about visits focused on his sex-offender status. First, a "friendly officer from the city police" came by for Duncan's quarterly offender check: "Each time they seem to add more and more to the check, this time they wanted ID and phone number." Then—"Here We Go Again"—a reporter from the local paper appeared, wanting to know "if I had any comment about the charges against me in Becker County for an article he is preparing for the paper tomorrow."

In an entry dated April 10, Duncan seemed to be edging toward some delusional state: "Bohemian Underground is Conceived. As I watch history unfold, I am compelled to help keep it on course."

Then, in an April 15 entry he became more defensive: "The Boogyman Will Get Ya:"

So, I've been accused of molesting a little boy. Those close to me know I didn't do it of course, how could I, I'm not even a pedophile. Well, I'm not a psychopath either, I feel the full force and pain of everyone I have ever hurt, but that doesn't stop me from doing what I need to do. Ultimately my feelings don't matter, I learned that in prison. I have to carry out my orders or a lot worse than just me dying could happen.

Ten days pass before his next entry, and it becomes clear that Duncan has gone deeper into his cycle, caught up in a "battle of epic proportions" with his demons: "Yes, I am still alive. I honestly wish not, I just don't know how to kill myself so it makes sense." Duncan described himself as "scared and alone" and wrote that being alone "is a fate that I probably chose sometime before I was ever born because I've been making the decision to fight my battles alone since I was a small child." He warned that his demons were stronger than ever, "taking my best blows and not even staggering," and that no one but God could help him:

> Only two people in the world have a clue as to the power and nature of my demons (besides me) and they will probably never read this. . . . I'm afraid, very afraid. If they (the demons) win then a lot of people will be badly hurt, and they've had their way before, so I know what they can do. I've been praying a lot and asking God for help. . . . If you are reading this, and you believe in God, please pray for God to help me defeat my demons. God has shown me the right choice, but my demons have me tied to a spit and the fire has already been lit. I don't know if the right choice is even an option anymore!

Duncan, at this point, was clearly alone in his battle of wits between what was right and wrong, yet he clearly seemed to know the difference. He appeared to be utilizing his blog as a means of crying out for help, and he invited strangers to intervene on his behalf because he obviously had no one else he could turn to. As he fell deeper into his psycho-sexual cycle in a downward spiral toward offending, he seemed unable to control himself any longer, and appeared to be on the verge of just letting go or giving in to his deep-seated desires.

For example, in a blog entry titled "The Demons Have Taken Over," dated Wednesday, May 11, 2005, Duncan thanked his online advisers but seemed to admit defeat:

> As far as letting God take care of the Demons, too late. They've locked up the "Happy Joe" person in the same dungeon that "Happy Joe" kept them in for so many years. Now they are loose and I am very afraid. From now on I may refer to "Happy Joe" as "Jet" (me) and the demons as "The Bogeyman."
>
> I *have* been asking God to help defeat the demons. In fact, last night I was on my knees begging him, crying out loud to him, to help me. He didn't answer, again. The problem is I am loosing [sic] my religion . . .

The demons, he went on, have persuaded him to question his religious convictions:

> . . . and that is how they got the key to the dungeon, and trapped me inside. . . .
>
> I am scared, alone, and confused, and my reaction is to strike out toward the perceived source of my misery, society. My intent is to harm society as much as I can, then die. As for the "Happy Joe" (Jet), well he was just a dream. The bogeyman was alive and happy long before Happy Joe.

In another passage from this lengthy entry, Duncan blamed his long prison experience for his rage:

> As an adult all I knew was the oppression of incarceration. All those years I dreamed of getting out . . . And getting even.

And when he did "get even" and did not "get caught," he started to see the possibility of a new life:

> Well that was when the "Happy Joe" dream started. I met a bunch of really great people, the kind of people I didn't even know existed, but here they were . . . my neighbors, my landlords, my professors, my coworkers, and they were all good people, who were willing to give me a chance despite my past.
>
> So, I tried to make it work.

But then his demons would return, "reminding me that if my new 'friends' knew about them (and what they, I, had done to even), then so much for their friendship. So, 'Happy Joe' was just dreaming, or pretending to be happy."

Duncan's final blog entry, believed to have been made from a laptop computer while he was either on his way to Idaho or already in Idaho, was dated Friday, May 13, 2005, the Friday before the brutal murders and child abductions. He titled it "Still Confused," and wrote that he didn't know whether "taking people with me"— presumably a reference to killing—was right or wrong.

> Does anything matter? My mother is crying right now, because her son is in trouble again. She tried to raise a good

son, and she knows her son has a good heart, so why does he do these things? . . . . It hurts me to know these things, but DOES IT MATTER??? A hundred year from now, all my mothers (sic) pain will be forgotten, and other mothers will cry for there (sic) sons. A million years from now there probably won't be any mothers (at least not like we know).

Duncan went on to portray himself as "more sensitive than most people," but prevented by his demons from expressing his caring feelings "for the starving children and families in the world." He also revealed that he was writing down his most honest feelings ("hundreds of times more frank than this blog could ever be") in an encrypted journal that some day—"I figure in 30 years or more"—would be decoded. Then "the world will know who I really was, and what I really did, and what I really thought. Also, maybe then they will understand that despite my actions, I'm not a bad person, I just have a disease contracted from society . . . . I hope to complete this journal before I die (soon) or turn myself in (I still might do that, I think it is the right thing, but of course, I'm not sure)."

Duncan's last blog entry makes it quite clear that, in his mind, whether conscious or subconscious, he was on a road of no return. He had made up his mind that he was going to complete his latest "cycle," and that there would be no turning back. He was blaming others, i.e., "society," for his actions and was not taking any responsibility for them. It was his "demons" that were in control, not him. In his mind, he was a good person who was "sensitive" and who had "feelings," more feelings than the average person. His "heart" was in the right place; he just couldn't control his "demons."

Duncan's writings were voluminous, and the detectives found themselves wondering what they would uncover as they read his written material. They also learned that he had an affinity for dressing in drag, and at one point in his life he had posted a series of such photos of himself on the Internet and labeled them "Jazzi Jet," apparently as an example of how he really viewed himself.

Detectives Maskell and Mattos still weren't sure just what they were dealing with here, but it was beginning to look more and more like Duncan's crimes went far beyond those he was suspected of committing in northern Idaho. They wanted to know how many times he had "gotten even," and where.

It was beginning to look like Duncan might be a serial killer.

—CHAPTER FOURTEEN—

STEVE GROENE WOULD LATER RECALL THAT WHEN HE'D left Coeur d'Alene on Friday evening, July 1, 2005, to travel to the Seattle area to visit his sister, he had no idea what had become of his children or whether he would ever see either of them again. He arrived at his sister's home at approximately 1 A.M. and about an hour into his visit he received a telephone call from the Kootenai County Sheriff's Department informing him that Shasta had been found, alive. He was very tired from the long drive, and was extremely grateful when a relative had offered to drive him back to Coeur d'Alene that morning.

"No sooner did he get here and go through the niceties, and the phone rings," said Groene's brother-in-law, Bob Price. "Needless to say, it was hugs and excitement."

At about 10 A.M. Groene arrived at the Kootenai Medical Center where Shasta had been admitted.

"When I walked in the door," Groene said, describing his reunion with his daughter to Geraldo Rivera, "her face just lit up, and she put her arms out and said, 'Daddy, Daddy!' It was one of the better moments of my life . . . She looks real good. She's very upbeat. . . . She seems to be in pretty good spirits . . . She acts just like the little girl I saw three weeks before she disappeared."

When asked by a reporter whether he had asked Shasta about her ordeal and what she had gone through before being rescued, Groene responded that he had not.

"She needs to address that on her own time, on her own terms," Groene said.

Groene spent most of the day and that night with Shasta, and found himself hoping that he would soon be having a similar reunion with Dylan.

"We still do have very high hopes," Groene said in response to the opinions of sheriff's department detectives and FBI agents who had begun to express their doubts about Dylan being found alive. "I would not give up hope anyway until I had absolute proof."

At one point amid all of the media attention that was being provided to this case, Oprah Winfrey, herself a victim of rape and molestations, jumped on the bandwagon and announced on her television show that she had launched a campaign to capture child molesters who had not yet been brought to justice. She offered a reward of $100,000 per case on her website, and posted the names and photographs, as well as descriptions of alleged offenses, of some of the most notorious sex criminals at large. Her motivation, it seems, stemmed from the fact that she had been raped by a 19-year-old cousin when she was only 9 and had also been molested by a family friend and a relative.

"With every breath in my body," Winfrey said, "whatever it takes, and most importantly, with your [the public's] support, we are going to move heaven and earth to stop a sickness, a darkness that I believe is the definition of evil . . . The children of this nation . . . are being stolen, raped, tortured and killed by sexual predators who are walking right into your homes. How many times does it have to happen?"

Two days later one of the fugitives pictured on Oprah's website was captured. The suspect faced charges of molesting three boys, and had a conviction of molestation that dated back to 1992.

Steve Groene expressed his support of Oprah's efforts, which were aimed not only at capturing sex criminals, but also at stiffening the laws for people who commit sex crimes, particularly those who commit offenses against children.

"I spoke with Oprah and she, like the rest of us, wants a change in the laws," Groene said. "Duncan's first offense was raping a fourteen-year-old boy and burning him with a cigarette. Why was he let out? Oprah's just sick of the laws in this country."

Although Shasta appeared to be doing well after her terrible ordeal, no one could see what was going on inside her. Of course, it didn't take a genius to figure out that she had a lot of feelings to deal with, such as grief and trauma, and that would take a lot of time. No one, at this point, could predict how she would reconcile her feelings internally.

"Often people say that young children are resilient," said Jenny Wieland, director of Families & Friends of Violent Crime Victims, based in Washington. "That's true, but they are extremely traumatized if they witness a violent crime."

No one knew just yet exactly what Shasta had experienced, both on the night of the abduction and later while being held captive. But based on what was being learned about Duncan, the investigators figured that she had been through a lot. Even though the police suspected at this point that Dylan was dead, they weren't speculating or telling the media what, if anything, they knew regarding what Shasta may have witnessed during the weeks that she had been gone.

"She's a little girl who's been through who knows what in the last six weeks," said Captain Ben Wolfinger.

"Being a victim undermines very basic human needs," Wieland said, "such as the need to feel safe, being able to trust and the ability to rebuild relationships." That all takes time, Wieland said. "[Shasta's experience isn't something] that she's ever going to get over."

According to the American Academy of Child and Adolescent Psychiatry, victims of violence or sexual abuse, such as Shasta, sometimes develop post-traumatic stress disorder, a condition that can consist of nightmares of her experiences, worrying about death, and difficulty concentrating and sleeping. In addition to emotional symptoms, some victims of post-traumatic stress disorder also develop physical symptoms or ailments when they are reminded of their terrible experience.

Polly Franks, a spokeswoman for the National Coalition for Victims in Action, expressed concern over all of the attention that Shasta was receiving from the media and the community where she lives.

"Part of it, I think, is unavoidable," Franks said, "because it is such a high-profile story. As much as humanly possible, she's going to need to fade back into the woodwork. She's going to have to have some form of normality."

Franks emphasized the importance of love and support for Shasta from her family and friends. She urged everyone to control their anger and the desire for revenge that many people were expressing, both privately and publicly, and to put their energies into determining how best to help Shasta deal with everything that she had gone through.

"As much as people want their pound of flesh from Duncan," Franks said, "the people around her are going to have to put her needs first."

"As we can imagine," said Shasta's uncle, Bob Price, "her psyche is pretty fragile at this point. . . . [But] she's a tough gal. She's a scrapper. She's got a lot of Groene in her. God knows what she's been through."

Shasta's father, as well as other relatives, expressed their gratitude to the community for the outpouring of concern, generosity and support that they'd shown for Shasta. She had received gifts of toys, as well as balloons and cards, many of which had come from her classmates and their families. School officials and others also bought new clothes for her and had them sent to her hospital room.

"I would especially like to thank all those involved in the search for Dylan and Shasta," said Steve Groene at yet another press conference. "A special thank you goes to the people at Denny's who were alert enough to recognize Shasta and make that 911 call. The Groene family truly feels you all are heroes."

"The staff is overjoyed [that Shasta was found alive]," said Coeur d'Alene Superintendent of Schools Harry Amend. "Now, of course, everyone is praying and talking about Dylan."

In the meantime, as the investigation focused on finding Dylan, Shasta began talking to the detectives. At first, they were tight-lipped about what she had told them, but she apparently provided sufficient information to support their earlier concerns.

"Based on the information that the investigators were able to put together," Wolfinger said, "it totally leads them to believe that Dylan is dead. That's why we are working so diligently right now to verify that, or find out that it's not true. . . . Frankly, I'd be more than happy to stand up here and say it's the biggest mistake we ever made, but unfortunately we don't think it's going to be."

In their efforts to determine the locations where Shasta and Dylan were being held against their will following their kidnapping, the detectives began looking at several locations in northern Idaho and Montana. Most of the information, they said, had been obtained from Shasta.

They had also begun looking into whether or not there was any connection between Joseph Edward Duncan III and any member of the Groene family. Shasta apparently told Maskell and Mattos that Duncan had described material that he had left behind in Fargo, North Dakota. It was not revealed what the material pertained to, and the details of such, depending upon their significance to the case, would be kept under wraps until trial. Although they had initially discounted any kind of connection between Duncan and the Groene family, they felt that it was a matter that had to be investigated, if for no other reason than to rule it out. The investigators flew to Fargo to search Duncan's apartment to determine if there was anything useful there that might help them in their case in Idaho.

Duncan, in the meantime, invoked his Fifth Amendment right against self-incrimination and refused to speak to the detectives.

—CHAPTER FIFTEEN—

It wasn't until a hearing, in which evidence and testimony was presented to Kootenai County Judge Scott Wayman, in an attempt to determine whether there was probable cause to charge Duncan with two counts of first-degree kidnapping, that details surrounding the killings and abductions began to emerge.

It was also the first time that the public was told that Dylan was indeed dead, and that Duncan had allegedly killed him.

Detective Brad Maskell explained to the judge how he had been called and informed that Shasta had been rescued at the Denny's in Coeur d'Alene and how her alleged abductor had been arrested. He also described his first encounter with Shasta when he went to the Kootenai Medical Center. Maskell said that he noticed some minor marks or scratches on her left arm, but that she otherwise appeared in good condition, at least physically. He said that when she spoke to him, she was clear and articulate.

According to details that were related to Detectives Maskell and Mattos, either by Shasta herself or through police officers who repeated what the girl had told them on the night she was rescued, Shasta and Dylan had been asleep in their bedrooms when the intruder, identified as Joseph Edward Duncan III, had entered their home on the night of May 15, 2005. Shasta's mother had called out to her from the living room, waking her up, and then called her into the living room where Shasta first saw Duncan. Shasta also saw her brother Slade, her mother and Mark McKenzie, each bound with duct tape and zip ties. Duncan, at one point, tied up Shasta and Dylan as well, and carried them outside, where he placed them inside a white pickup truck that had been parked on the property. He then returned to the house to kill the children's family. Shasta said that Duncan had been wearing dark gloves that night.

Shasta, according to Maskell, told the investigators in their preliminary interviews that Duncan had entered the house through the back door and that he was armed with what she described as a rifle or a long gun. Since Shasta had been asleep at the time that he entered the house, she had not initially known how Duncan got inside. It was revealed that he had later explained to her and her brother how he'd gained entry to the home. After she and Dylan had been bound and gagged and taken outside to the pickup truck, and after Duncan had gone back inside the house, she said that she heard Mark McKenzie cry out in pain before everything went silent.

At another point, according to Maskell, Shasta said that she saw Slade come outside. Of the three victims, he had been the only one whose feet had not been bound. He was severely injured when Shasta saw him, with a deep head wound and bleeding severely. She believed, in her words, that "he was brain dead."

According to media reports of the probable cause hearing that quickly began showing up on newsstands and television screens, Shasta vividly recalled the smallest details of the night that her family was killed. Although Shasta had told the investigators that she and her brother had not witnessed the actual murders, she explained how Duncan had shown them a hammer and how he'd told them that he had used it to kill their family members. Shasta even recalled the brand name of the claw hammer—a FatMax.

According to Maskell, investigators had purchased a FatMax hammer and were able to match the tool markings on it to the wounds on the victims' skulls.

Shasta said that during the time that she and her brother were held captive, Duncan had told her during their many conversations how he'd committed the crime against her family. He explained to her how he had been driving by one day and saw her and her brother playing outside, and how Shasta had been wearing a bathing suit at the time.

"He told her he watched her two or three days," Maskell told the judge, "and at night would peer inside the home." Maskell said that Duncan had used night-vision goggles to learn the home's floor plan before making his move.

According to the story that Shasta related, he drove his stolen vehicle, the red Jeep Cherokee, over to the Hollingsworth property and parked it by one of the outbuildings. It was at night, so he took a flashlight and walked across the field to Shasta's home, where he found that the back door had been left unlocked and ajar. When the residents' dogs approached him and began barking, he pointed the gun at them, and his motions frightened the dogs away.

Duncan had obtained the keys to the pickup from Mark McKenzie, and had also taken McKenzie's wallet. After committing the killings, Duncan drove Shasta and Dylan in the white pickup across the field to Hollingsworth's property, where he parked it. He then transferred the children into the stolen Jeep and left the area with them.

Shasta said she believed that the man, who sometimes referred to himself as "Jet," had taken her and her brother to Montana. She thought it was in Montana where the man had held them captive because he had shown her the area on a map. She described the area as the Lolo Forest, and they had stayed at a campsite that was located a considerable distance from the freeway. She said that they had been at that campsite for quite some time, that they had been there "ever since." She also spoke of "things" that had occurred at the campsite. Over the next few weeks, she described in a child's voice and language how both she and Dylan were repeatedly molested by Duncan.

While at the campsite, Shasta said that Duncan had photographed himself with her and Dylan, apparently with a video camera. Duncan, the detectives knew, had liked to use video because they had seen some creative postings of his videos that he had placed on a website. One in particular had been made a couple of years ago at Thanksgiving time at someone's home. There were children and adults present who were photographed, but that video in particular seemed to focus more on the children than anything else. As for the video that was allegedly made at the Montana campsite, it was described as very disturbing and offensive. Maskell said that Duncan had apparently shown some of it to Shasta.

"She has actually seen in the viewfinder of the camera some of the pictures that he has taken," Maskell told the judge, "that depict her and Dylan actually with Mr. Duncan during the period of time that they were held captive."

Shasta also told Maskell that Duncan had related to her many sordid details of how he had sexually molested her brother. He had even tortured the boy, burning him with cigarettes, and eventually killed him by shooting him with a shotgun, according to Maskell's testimony.

The hearing had been Duncan's first court appearance with regard to the case, and it was made via video feed. Throughout the hearing Duncan kept his gaze downward, and his lower lip trembled occasionally. He was seen swallowing hard several times, and it appeared as if he was attempting to remain composed. Duncan was appointed a public defender, Lynn Nelson, and he was asked by the judge if he understood the charges that he was facing.

"I believe I do, yes," Duncan responded.

The kidnapping charges were very specific in that they accused Duncan of keeping Shasta and Dylan confined and captive for the express purposes of raping them and otherwise causing them serious bodily harm during the course of sexually molesting them.

Judge Wayman ordered Duncan held without bail on the kidnapping charges, and set bail at $2 million on the fugitive warrant.

Chief Deputy Prosecutor Lansing Haynes made it

clear that Duncan might face murder charges, as well as various other charges, as the results of the ongoing investigation became known.

"As more facts come to light," Haynes said, "this office will make some decisions based on those facts."

As additional facts began to surface, it became crystal clear that Duncan was a violent sex offender who should never have been set free.

—CHAPTER SIXTEEN—

As the investigators dug into Duncan's background, from his criminal records in various jurisdictions as well as his prison records and reports of his psychological evaluations, they learned that there were conflicting reports with regard to where he was born. One version indicated that he was born on February 25, 1963, in New Orleans, Louisiana, to Joseph E. Duncan Jr. and Lillian Mae Duncan. Another indicated that he was born in Fort Bragg, North Carolina, and yet a third showed that he was born in Tacoma, Washington—and was also raised there. As they pieced the case together, it appeared that Tacoma was the correct choice.

He apparently told one of his prison therapists that his first sexual experience occurred in 1971 when he was 8 years old—sexual contact allegedly was made by two young female relatives. He purportedly told his therapist that four years later, in 1975, he'd sexually assaulted a 5-year-old boy, and in 1978, had done the same thing to a 9-year-old boy in Tacoma, at gunpoint this time.

In 1979 Duncan was arrested following a high-speed chase in a car that he had stolen and in which he had attempted to run through a police roadblock. He crashed the car and sustained injuries to the right side of his face, requiring reconstructive surgery. He was sent to the Dyslin boys' ranch in Tacoma for several months, where he told a therapist that he had bound and sexually assaulted six boys, and estimated thirteen rapes of younger boys, by the time he was 16. He dropped out of Lakes High School in Lakewood, Washington, when he was in the tenth grade.

On January 24, 1980, when Duncan was nearly 17, he broke into a neighbor's home and stole a gun. The details of that case had disturbing similarities to the details that Shasta had provided to investigators. According to police and prosecution reports, Duncan had abducted a 14-year-old boy who was walking to school. Wielding the gun, Duncan took the boy into a wooded area where he forced him to undress and perform a sex act on him. Afterward he took the boy deeper into the woods and sexually assaulted him again. When he had finished, he beat the boy's buttocks with a piece of wood and burned him with a cigarette. He then took the boy back to where he had left his clothes, allowed him to dress, and instructed the boy to run away. Duncan was arrested that evening, and was eventually sentenced to 20 years in prison.

In May 1980 Duncan was admitted to Western State Hospital's sexual psychopath program for treatment. There were at least two occasions that Duncan, while staying at an extended visit facility where he could be with family members, would sneak out at night while his family was asleep, to prowl the neighborhood and peep into the windows of several nearby homes. He was also caught masturbating in public during these visits.

It was clear to his therapists that he was making a conscious choice at not controlling himself. "He has chosen not to commit himself to our program," his therapists wrote. Because he continued with his sexually deviant behavior, Duncan was deemed "not amenable to treatment" and was sent back to prison to serve out the remainder of his original sentence.

During the course of his incarceration, Duncan was moved in and out of protective custody because other inmates were frequently pressuring him for sexual favors. There were also several incidents where he was placed in disciplinary segregation, usually for ten days at a time, for infractions that were the result of contraband found inside his cell during shakedowns. The contraband included such items as needles, wires, razor blades, a VCR and two videotapes. Although he claimed that the VCR and videotapes were borrowed from his "employment" at the prison, it was determined that the two tapes contained pornography. He had also gotten into trouble for ordering publications through the mail that promoted child pornography, including bondage and homosexual activities with children.

By November 1989, Duncan wrote to parole officials and said that he had made an "important decision to explore my feminine traits." He also began a pen-pal correspondence with David Woelfert, a male King County revenue department employee, who also began talking to Duncan on the telephone and who sometimes traveled from his home near Tacoma to visit Duncan at the state prison in Walla Walla, some 270 miles away. Woelfert eventually became something of a sponsor of Duncan's, and wrote to the parole review board on Duncan's behalf.

"Mr. Duncan is filled with remorse for the act that he committed many years ago," Woelfert wrote in letters in the early 1990s. "Further incarceration of Mr. Duncan will serve no purpose whatsoever." The friend was one of several whom Duncan would manipulate into taking actions on his behalf over the ensuing years. Duncan was paroled in 1994.

In January 1996, Duncan told his parole officer that he was "exploring" a relationship with a married woman who had two small children. She was one of Duncan's co-workers who had agreed to "helping him explore his feminine side" by understanding his transsexual fantasies and by assisting him with the selection and purchase of women's clothing so that he could dress in drag.

There were clearly multiple sides of Joseph Duncan emerging. On the one hand he was a flaming drag queen who had transsexual fantasies, and on the other he was a homosexual who appeared to have difficulty coming out. He could also obtain trust and praise from others, and excel at his work when he wanted to. An example of the latter was a temporary job he held at a software company as a technical support representative, where he again manipulated someone to come to his aid. One of the managers at the company wrote a letter of recommendation for Duncan:

Out of 30 temporary reps that I hired during the holiday season, Joe stands out as one of the best all-around performers, and I would not hesitate to hire him again.

Because of Duncan's growing openness and acceptance of his gay tendencies, his therapist took him on a retreat for male homosexuals at Leavenworth, Washington, where she could observe first-hand how he interacted with other gay men. Later that same year, in July 1996, Duncan moved in with a gay couple, but would later tell his parole officer that he planned to "give up his homosexuality and attend to heterosexual experiences."

A short time later, Duncan violated his parole by using marijuana and getting caught, and for possession of a firearm. There were also several instances where he failed to obtain permission from his parole officer before visiting relatives and other people who had minor children in their homes. He was sent to jail for 30 days, and then released.

During that same timeframe, July 1996, Sammiejo White, 11, and Carmen Cubias, 9, half sisters from Seattle, were last seen leaving a motel room near the downtown area where they had been staying. Duncan was living and working in the Bothell, Washington, area, 15 miles away, at that time. The girls' bodies were found in a field nearly two years later, in February 1998, in Bothell. Although Duncan had not been initially viewed as a suspect in the case, it seemed prudent to take a good hard look at him now in light of the circumstances surrounding Shasta and Dylan Groene. His background and movements from that point on were carefully scrutinized, particularly where missing and murdered children were involved. Following his arrest in Idaho during Shasta's rescue, Duncan purportedly discussed Sammiejo's and Carmen's deaths, and told FBI agents who were interviewing him that he had killed the two little girls.

"Duncan didn't remember their names," said an FBI agent. But he reportedly provided enough information

that the agents had been able to conclude that he was referring to Sammiejo White and Carmen Cubias.

As MASKELL AND MATTOS, AS WELL AS THE FEDERAL IN-
vestigators who were working on the case, looked
more closely at the details surrounding Sammiejo White
and Carmen Joy Cubias, they learned that the girls had
disappeared at approximately 8:30 P.M. on Saturday, July
6, 1996, after leaving the Crest Motel, located at North
141st Street and Aurora Avenue North, to purchase cigarettes at a nearby store for an older brother. The two girls
often played in the motel's parking lot without supervision. Their remains were found on Tuesday, February 10,
1998, buried at the edge of a field on a hillside on an
abandoned farm in Bothell. A transient who had been living in the farm's barn had discovered the girls' remains
and led a Bothel police officer to three leg bones and a
foot bone that had apparently been unearthed and scat-
tered about by construction work being done at the farm.
Following four days of intensive searching in the muddy
field, investigators found approximately seventy bones,
including a skull with teeth, and a jaw with a partial set
of teeth. Dental records and the size or stature of their
bones helped investigators identify the girls' remains, as
did their clothing.

Sammiejo had been wearing a yellow long-sleeved
turtleneck sweater, white T-shirt and blue jeans, and Carmen had been dressed in a black T-shirt and pink stretch
pants when they disappeared. Their mother came home
at about 10 P.M. and discovered that the girls were missing. She spent the next few hours looking for them, and

finally reported them missing to Seattle police at 2 A.M.

When detectives interviewed the girls' mother, they were told that the two were very independent in nature. They often traveled the Seattle area by bus, and had become very familiar with the area as well as with the bus system and how to use it effectively. They had only lived in the area for about a year, having moved there from the Tri-Cities (Kennewick, Pasco and Richland) in eastern Washington in 1995, the same year that their mother had given birth to her ninth child.

"Neither girl had any money," their mother told detectives. "But they knew how to panhandle."

Their mother said that she paid the rent on their motel room with donations that they received from a local charity.

Investigators working the case at the time had been able to determine that the girls likely died of "homicidal violence" a short time after they had disappeared, a determination that had been made with the assistance of a forensic anthropologist.

"The death certificate was signed, after we made the identification, as 'a homicidal violence of undetermined etiology,'" said the anthropologist. "The reason we were able to say it was a homicidal death was because we had nothing but bone fragments, and no other logical conclusion could be drawn—nine- and eleven-year-old girls do not die and then bury their own bodies."

As the investigators tried to confirm Duncan's story of killing the two half sisters, some of the facts appeared to match Duncan's "confession," including the fact that he had lived near the motel where the girls were living when they disappeared. Despite the fact that Duncan's confession appeared in the *Coeur d'Alene Press*, with the paper quoting an unidentified source close to the investigation, it is important to note that sometimes a suspected killer's confession turns out to be bogus.

"Duncan's confession could be like some of those other serial killers who have claimed credit for things they haven't done," said an FBI agent.

Duncan was not a suspect at the time the girls' disappearance was being investigated. Detective Dennis Nizzi of the Bothell Police Department retired from police work in 1999, leaving the case unsolved. He characterized it as the most frustrating case of his twenty-seven-year police career.

"We had never heard of Duncan," Nizzi said recently. "There were no solid suspects in the case. I handled a lot of major crimes and homicides in my career, and I can say that no one wants to walk away from a crime of this magnitude unsolved. It has troubled me."

A major burden of that case was that too much time had passed from the time the girls disappeared until the time that their remains were found.

"The bodies had completely decomposed," Nizzi said. "We had nothing but one-and-one-half-year-old bones. . . . If there is something that comes out of Mr. Duncan's mouth and it solves the crime, I will be tickled to death. I will be the first in court to watch this happen. I would love to see this case get cleared."

Sergeant John Urquhart, spokesperson for the King County Sheriff's Office, told reporters that there was no physical evidence linking Duncan to the killing of Sammiejo and Carmen. Urquhart indicated that there were many police agencies in the region that were in the process

of reviewing their cold cases involving child kidnapping
and homicide following Duncan's arrest. But he was skep-
tical whether any of these could be pinned on Duncan.

"We have not talked to Joe Duncan," Urquhart said.
"We did send detectives over there [to Idaho] to follow up.
But he lawyered up, and we have not interviewed him."

Urquhart said that he could not confirm what the
newspapers had been reporting, namely that Duncan
had admitted that he had killed Sammiejo and Carmen.

"I'm not going to deny it, but I'm not going to confirm it either," Urquhart said of the reported admissions.
"Serial killers oftentimes confess to crimes they didn't
commit. That doesn't mean he doesn't know who did
it. . . . We don't have anything yet that conclusively
links him to this [double] homicide. He has not con-
fessed to us."

At the time of this writing, the FBI was working to
put together a comprehensive list of Duncan's movements around the country. So far Duncan is known to
have visited Washington, Idaho, Montana, Wyoming,
North Dakota, Minnesota, Wisconsin, Michigan, Missouri, Florida, California and possibly Nevada while on
parole status. At the present time he is known or suspected of committing crimes in Washington, Idaho,
Montana, California and Minnesota.

—CHAPTER SEVENTEEN—

DUNCAN'S BACKGROUND CONTINUED TO BE OF MAJOR IN-terest to investigators from every law enforcement agency working on the Shasta and Dylan Groene case. It appeared that Duncan had failed a number of polygraphs regarding contact with minor children during the early months of 1997. Apparently fearing that he would be sent back to prison for the infractions, he cut off commu-nications with his parole officer by claiming that he was staying at his mother's house in Tacoma, and that his car was not working. A short time later he disappeared, tak-ing with him a girlfriend's 1986 Chrysler New Yorker. When his parole officer visited Duncan's mother, she claimed that she had last seen her son on March 31, 1997, and did not know his current whereabouts.

Only days earlier, on March 26, 1997, in Oak Harbor, Washington, 7-year-old Deborah Palmer was last seen walking to Oak Harbor Elementary School at approxi-mately 8:35 A.M. That same day Duncan had an appoint-ment to undergo a polygraph examination in Seattle, 92 miles south of Oak Harbor. It was a ninety-minute drive from where Deborah had last been seen. Deborah's partially clad body was found five days later, on March 31, after it washed up on a beach approximately five miles from where she'd disappeared. Although it was determined that Deborah had not been sexually molested, the cops investigating her case considered her death to be sexually motivated because of the nature of the crime—she was strangled—and because of the fact that her body was only partially clothed when it was found.

During the timeframe in which Duncan disappeared, police learned that he may have visited a relative in southern California. There were also indications that he may have visited his father, who by then resided in a retirement community called Pahrump in southern Nevada. Pahrump is located about 50 miles from Las Vegas on the California–Nevada border, about a four-and-one-half-hour drive to the Los Angeles area. Although they had not yet been able to substantiate it, the cops had reason to believe that Duncan may have traveled to Highland, California, located about 22 miles from Beaumont, to visit the relative who lived there. This would have placed him in the southern California area, or at least in close proximity to it, during the first few days of April 1997.

When the detectives began checking for any criminal activity in that particular area that may have fit Duncan's profile, they soon learned that 10-year-old Anthony Martinez had been kidnapped by a "mustached man" in Beaumont on April 4, 1997. Martinez had been playing with his younger brother and several friends in an alley behind their home when a man approached the boys and offered them money to help him find his lost cat.

"He first went after Anthony's brother, but that boy got away," said Beaumont Police Lieutenant Mitch White. "He got Anthony."

According to Anthony's brother's statement to the police, the man threatened Anthony with a knife and forced him into a white 1986 Chrysler New Yorker sedan and drove away. The car's description matched a description of Duncan's girlfriend's car that was provided to police by a neighbor.

Anthony's bound, naked body was found fifteen days later, on April 19, in a shallow grave in a remote area near Berdoo Canyon, located east of Palm Springs, just off of a road that leads to Joshua Tree National Park. As in the northern Idaho case, duct tape had been used in binding Anthony's body. According to the autopsy report, Anthony had been sexually assaulted. A wanted poster that was circulated in southern California at the time of Anthony's death depicted a suspect who bore a striking resemblance to Duncan.

Detectives Maskell and Mattos recalled from their trip to Fargo, North Dakota, that Duncan was a cat fancier who had kept two cats at his Fargo apartment, and had abandoned them when he fled that area. When they had searched his apartment they found that he had also posted photos of his cats on his various Internet sites.

All of the information was shared between the agencies, and at one point Duncan agreed to speak with FBI agents. During the questioning, he mentioned Anthony Martinez's name. The FBI contacted Riverside County, California, Sheriff Bob Doyle about the Martinez case.

"It was a situation where they were asking him about his involvement in any other similar case," Doyle told a reporter with the *National Enquirer*. "He said, 'Yeah, this boy Martinez in southern California, Riverside

County.' It was not a full, blown-out confession, though. We need more. . . .

"The FBI asked us if we knew anything about a Martinez case. I said, 'We sure do—we've been trying to solve the murder for the last eight years and we've gone through fifteen thousand leads.' So when we were able to match a partial [right] thumb print on duct tape found near Anthony's body with that of Duncan, we knew we had our man."

Although Doyle sent investigators to the Kootenai County jail in Coeur d'Alene to interview Duncan, it was to no avail—Duncan refused to speak with them.

"We haven't charged him yet, but we intend to carry out further investigations," Doyle said. "And we certainly are looking to interview him again."

Anthony's mother, upon learning of the circumstances of Duncan's parole after serving 14 years of a 20-year sentence, was furious—and rightfully so.

"How do you get out for good behavior?" she asked. "Someone like that can't be rehabilitated. I don't care what psychologists say."

Upon linking Duncan to Anthony's death, the FBI began looking into the possibility that there might be other murders that could be linked to Duncan that had so far gone unsolved.

"For all we know, there may be a whole string of bodies out there," a source with law enforcement told a reporter. "We just don't know."

As they continued piecing together their timeline, Maskell and Mattos learned that Duncan had traveled east and ended up at his half sister's house in Kansas City, Missouri. Because of parole violations and, specifically, because he failed to register as a sex offender there, the FBI tracked him down. When they showed up at the door, Duncan answered and was arrested on the spot. He was promptly returned to prison in Washington state where he soon began propositioning other inmates for sex. When they refused his advances, he would become angry and threatening toward them. He was placed in administrative segregation. One of the propositioned inmates wrote the following letter to prison authorities:

> Inmate Duncan has been pressuring me for sexual favors since my first day in his cell. First he started off by saying, "I don't care what you heard about me in the yard, but I *only* take it in the ass." Saturday night we took a shower together and afterward he was offering me a massage. I made it very clear to him I was not interested and he started to get mad. He was offended by my rejection. He said that I had to sleep sometime. . . .

During his latest round of incarceration in Washington state, Duncan was charged with fighting with his cellmate, a minor infraction considering the violence involved in the crimes that had landed him in prison in the first place. Duncan, in an apparent blunder on his part, initiated the contact with corrections officials that resulted in him being charged with fighting.

According to the reports, on February 14, 1999, Duncan apparently reported to corrections officers that he had been having a problem with a fellow inmate at the facility, similar to a halfway house, where they were required to live. When his cellmate was questioned, he said that it was Duncan who had the problem. His cellmate said that Duncan's hygiene was poor, and that he had merely questioned Duncan at one point about when he was going to make his bed. Duncan apparently had the bunk above his cellmate's. According to the cellmate, Duncan, in a fit of anger, threw a cup of coffee on him. If Duncan had kept his mouth shut, it is likely that nothing would have come out of the incident. As it was, Duncan was found guilty of the infraction. In his appeal, Duncan wrote a letter on February 19, 1999, which clearly showed that he was capable of attempting to manipulate the system, and did not easily accept responsibility for his actions.

"I do not understand how I was found guilty, nor am I clear on exactly what I was found guilty of," Duncan declared at the start of the letter, complaining that the only evidence against him was his cellmate's accusation. "So, if there is any other evidence or statements against me (I assume there is/are none) then let me point out that I have not received any opportunity to refute them, as I know I could since I did *nothing* wrong. I did not even attempt to defend myself in this 'altercation.'"

Duncan argued that the physical evidence in the case supported his version of what happened, not his cellmate's. He explained how his shirt was torn, allegedly by his cellmate, when he was attempting to escape his cellmate's purported violence against him. He claimed that his cellmate struck him twice, causing "red marks" on his face and neck. He stated that the red marks were observed by a corrections officer as well as by hospital staff.

According to Duncan, he did not "throw" coffee at his cellmate but was simply holding a cup of coffee when the cellmate hit *him*: "I don't think it would be reasonable to assume that anyone could hold onto a full cup of coffee while being hit full force in the jaw. Consequently my coffee was 'thrown' *everywhere*. On me, on the wall next to me, on *my* personal clothes hanging nearby, but mostly on the floor." If the cellmate also got coffee on him, Duncan added, "I would not be surprised considering his proximity, and if he hit me the *second* time because he got coffee on him then I don't see how I can be held accountable. . . ."

Duncan also denied engaging in a "heated exchange of words" with his cellmate on the morning in question. He stated that, in fact, he had decided not to make his bed the morning of the incident because he was attempting to avoid a confrontation with his cellmate, whose bed was directly below Duncan's and might be disturbed.

"A careful examination of the evidence and facts in this case can only support my statement," Duncan concluded. He claimed that he was the victim of an "unprovoked" attack and that he could produce letters that he had written to Dr. Richard Wacksman, his sponsor, about his cellmate's propensity for verbal and physical confrontation: "Dr. Wacksman will testify that in both letters and phone conversations he was aware of the extreme efforts" Duncan had made to avoid such confrontations.

At the close of the letter, Duncan begged for "justice" and for consideration of the "far reaching implications" of a fighting infraction in his case: "I am Pre-SRA (Sentencing Reform Act) and in for a violent sex-offense. I am very acutely aware of the potential consequences of a violent infraction." Because of those consequences, Duncan insisted, he refused to fight with his cellmate, even after being hit, and remained calm.

"Please take the time to investigate this incident," the letter ended. "I did nothing to even provoke [my cellmate]. Thank you. Joseph Duncan, #2875."

Despite his effort with the appeal, Duncan's infraction for being found guilty of fighting was allowed to stand and he was sentenced to ten days of segregation. In denying Duncan's appeal, the official statement read as follows:

> Your letter of appeal and related documents have been forwarded to me by the disciplinary clerk for review and response as Superintendent's designee. I have reviewed the material.
>
> You have appealed the finding of guilt based on your contention that you did not fight with another inmate, not even in self-defense. You claim you were the victim of an unprovoked attack by another inmate.
>
> A physical confrontation occurred between you and your cell partner. Staff did not witness this altercation. Your cell partner testified that the altercation ensued after you threw coffee on him. This is considered fighting with another person.
>
> I uphold the finding of guilt and the sanction assigned.

The letter was signed by Dennis Thaut, the superintendent's designee.

Two years earlier, the detectives learned, in December 1997, Duncan had been placed in administrative segregation, apparently because of some concern for his safety if he were to be retained in his current unit. At the time, Duncan was on parole suspension for absconding. His prison records showed that the coffee incident in 1999 was not his first run-in with a cellmate. According to official reports, Duncan had caused a similar situation between himself and another cellmate by complaining that the cellmate "smelled." Afterward the cellmate apparently grabbed him and would not let him go. According to Duncan, the inmate was trying to push him into reacting against him. Again, in Duncan's words, the altercation was not Duncan's fault. He stated that he did not know what the problem with the other inmate was, even though it was determined later that Duncan had insulted him about the way he smelled. Apparently the other inmate had stopped taking showers about five days earlier, and Duncan had become upset over his hygiene.

Throughout much of Duncan's prison life, he was employed inside the walls as a teacher's aide in the electronics shop. As part of his experience, in addition to classes taken in prison, he earned nearly enough credits to obtain an Associate of Technical Arts degree in electronics. He was only five credits short of earning the degree. He was not involved in any one-to-one counseling or group therapy. He spent much of his spare time watching television, but eventually became interested and involved in computer programming. He also liked to watch X-rated tapes, but could not seem to get away with doing so without getting caught. Each time he was caught with pornography he received 10 days' disciplinary segregation. He was labeled a high risk to reoffend.

On another occasion, during a routine shakedown, a large quantity of wire, assorted radio jacks spliced into each other, a large piece of wood and a baseball were found and confiscated. It is not known what Duncan intended to use the contraband items for, but he received 10 days' disciplinary segregation, suspended for 90 days provided that no further major infractions occurred. A short time later Duncan filed a grievance against a corrections officer, alleging that the officer had stolen a calculator from his room. An investigation, however, determined that Duncan had used the allegation against the officer in an attempt to remove him from his unit. It was determined that Duncan had maliciously filed a grievance with the intent of having formal disciplinary action taken against the correctional officer. Duncan received 10 days' disciplinary segregation and loss of 30 days of conduct time for the incident. The 10 days' disciplinary segregation appeared to be the cookie-cutter punishment for major infractions.

Going backwards through his prison records, the investigators learned that prison officials discovered while processing outgoing mail that Duncan had written a letter to David "Pumpkin" Woelfert on April 18, 1993, with instructions to make copies of a "fixed" Department of Corrections document and to destroy the original. Woelfert, it turned out, was a man Duncan had befriended who had agreed to sponsor him upon Duncan's parole. The document that Duncan had altered was a record of earned early release in which Duncan had cut out the word "Rape" under *Crime* and had replaced it with the word "Assault." It was obviously an attempt to forge official documentation with the intent to misrepresent his crime. His request to

Woelfert to make copies of the altered document and to destroy the original was clearly Duncan's intent to involve Woelfert in illegal activity.

Duncan's letter to Woelfert began:

> Dear Pumpkin,
> I Love You!
> Well, another week is gone! That's another week closer to you and me! I've been imagining what your lips are going to feel like on that very first great big kiss! Hey? Do you like to French?

Duncan told Woelfert how happy he was following a telephone conversation between the two men. He referred to a "special event" that Woelfert's father had attended in which a plaque had been presented to Woelfert and his brother. Duncan was not specific about the purpose of the event, but said that he wished he could have been there as Woelfert's "friend."

Then, after instructing Woelfert to send him two copies of the "fixed" printout and to "destroy the original," Duncan complained about his new cellmate—"one of those people who are afraid of peace and quiet" and produce as much noise as possible by having the television and the radio turned on at the same time. Duncan also told Woelfert that he thought he had caught a cold and was planning to spend more time resting in an effort to combat it. He closed by saying:

> I love you more and more all the time!
> Love, Joseph.

In response to the serious infraction report that was filed after Duncan's letter to "Pumpkin" was discovered, Duncan responded:

> I'm not guilty because it's not an official document. It is not signed nor is it sealed, therefore, I cannot get in trouble for altering it. I changed it to protect myself so people would not know what my crime was. I could have made this myself. It came off a dot matrix printer. It's not an official document.

Duncan received 5 days' segregation for the altered document.

As the detectives looked further into Duncan's background during his incarceration in the late 1990s, they learned more about the significance of his relationship with Dr. Wacksman, which he'd referred to in his appeal letter.

At one point, though the details were sketchy, it appeared that Duncan had spent some time in the San Francisco area prior to his trip to southern California. Although he had lived mostly on the streets, he'd apparently befriended Dr. Richard Wacksman, a physician who was there on vacation. Wacksman, who had lived in Harwood, North Dakota, about ten miles north of Fargo, now lives in Florida. After Duncan had fled Fargo, Wacksman was interviewed by Fargo police investigator Greg Esposito about his connection to Duncan. Wacksman explained that he had last spoken to Duncan on or around April 15, 2005, when Duncan had called him.

Wacksman, according to the police report that was filed in Fargo, had loaned him $6,500 prior to Duncan's

Becker County court appearances in Detroit Lakes, Minnesota, where he had been charged with molesting the 6-year-old boy and attempting to molest the boy's 8-year-old friend at the playground. The money, according to records, was intended to help defray Duncan's attorneys' fees. Duncan, however, had come up with the needed bail with help from another individual he had manipulated into believing that he was a friend. The "friend," a local businessman, Joe Crary, had borrowed the needed bail money and had loaned it to Duncan. When asked to make a statement about the loan, Crary wrote:

I, Joe Crary, am giving this statement concerning my connections with Joe Duncan. We both enjoyed biking on the bike trails in Fargo and we became acquaintances. In my contact with him, I saw him like many others apparently did—he was polite, soft spoken, and seemed sincere in turning his life around. He was working on his college degree and holding down two jobs at the same time. He was having some financial problems and I was trying to help him get things straightened out, just like I have tried to help many others over the years. After he posted bail in Becker County with his personal check for $15,000, he drove back to Fargo and called later that day and asked me for a loan to cover the check. I was aware that he had been served with a summons by mail about 40 days prior to the hearing. Duncan had actually gone to Kansas City after receiving the summons and came back prior to the hearing. So I naturally thought if he was going to run from the charges he would have already done so. Furthermore, he assured me he was innocent of the charges in Becker

County. So, in the end, I borrowed him the $15,000. I talked to him briefly after that two or three times before he left the area. He never mentioned to me that he had any intent of leaving the area. I have nothing else to say concerning Joe Duncan, and this is my complete and only statement I will make on this matter.

By the time he had telephoned Wacksman for the last time, Duncan had already fled Fargo and was actually already on the lam. According to available reports, Wacksman, a pediatrician, had allowed Duncan to visit him at his home in Florida in March 2005.

Backtracking the timeline, however, the investigators learned that Wacksman had contacted Duncan's parole officer several times on Duncan's behalf when Duncan lived in Fargo and Wacksman lived in Harwood. At one point Wacksman had asked the parole board in Washington to release Duncan so that Duncan could live at home with him and his wife and two kids, ages 8 and 11, stating that he had no concerns regarding the safety of his children. Wacksman wrote that he did not believe Duncan was homicidal.

Mr. Duncan is not much of a threat to society. He was a screwed-up adolescent that grew up in prison. . . . my work as a physician executive and co-chair of our corporate ethics committee has taught me to take risks and to do what is right.

The parole review board, under the direction of Chairwoman Kathryn "Kit" Bail, rejected Wacksman's proposal.

"Under no circumstances whatsoever would the board allow Mr. Duncan to reside in a home where victim age children reside," Bail wrote in the board's official decision. Although Bail wrote that Dr. Wacksman had indicated that he "feels that he can help Joe . . ." and even though Dr. Wacksman's wife was supportive of the proposal, ". . . I told Dr. Wacksman that we are unconcerned about his relationship with Joe, except insofar as it bears on his case or a potential parole plan. . . . With all due respect to Dr. Wacksman, we are not willing to expose his children to that kind of risk."

Washington had a law on its books that would allow the Department of Corrections to deny release indefinitely to a prisoner who had served his sentence, if he was adjudged to be a sexual predator. But the department's sentence review committee determined that Duncan did not qualify as a sexual predator, despite his extensive past and own admissions of molesting and raping children, and despite the fact that he had violated his parole on several previous occasions and had been returned to prison to finish out his original sentence of 20 years. Therefore, the state of Washington released Duncan in July 2000 with no supervision and no responsibilities—they only required him to register as a sex offender, despite the fact that the following report, one of many, was on file with the Board of Prison Terms and Paroles:

He [Duncan] has already served some 2 years at Western State [Hospital], where he has been categorized as a sexual psychopath, not safe to be at large and not amenable to treatment. The reports indicate that his deviant sexual history goes back to when he was 12 years old when he was involved with a five-year-old minor male. After that there are other incidents involving minor children whom he forced to [perform] fellatio [on] him, and according to their report, he also performed anal intercourse on the victims. By his own statement according to the report we have, he has committed approximately 13 different rapes on minor mails [sic]. He is seen as an extremely dangerous deviant.

Also in the files was a statement made by Duncan himself regarding the offense of raping the 14-year-old boy at gunpoint, which was incorporated as part of his End of Sentence Review psychological report. He explained that the rape had occurred because he was feeling abandoned. His older sisters had left home, his younger brother had moved in with his father, and his mother had gone out on a date. Duncan said:

> I noticed the old man that lived nearby wasn't at home. I also remembered he had guns, hand guns. So I prepared myself and went to a dark spot and broke in through a window. I then went to his room where I found a locked closet. I took the hinges off, and left with the guns and some money and some porno magazines. When I got back to my house, I had the guns and went in my room to masturbate to the porno material. Then, I decided, 'Why not [do] the real thing.' So I got a gun, unloaded, without a clip, and went cruising for a victim. I spotted my victim in front of [an elementary school]. I approached him with the gun and told him to go a certain spot in some woods. There I forced him to take off his clothes, and I sucked him and he sucked me. I came in his mouth. Then, I told him to get dressed and we walked one half mile to a different spot. The same

[thing] occurred except [that] I hit him a few times with a stick, and burnt him with a cigarette. Then I left him to get dressed, and when I got home I was arrested.

Duncan, following his eventual parole from Washington state, was placed on a bus bound for Seattle. However, he eventually made his way to North Dakota, and continued his friendship with Dr. Wacksman. Upon his arrival in Fargo, Duncan showed up at the police department and registered as a sex offender and was classified Level III.

People who lived in Wacksman's Harwood neighborhood were not at all happy with the fact that he was allowing a Level III sex offender to spend time there, particularly when some of their children were friends with Wacksman's.

"We had a neighborhood meeting about it," recalled one of the residents. They confronted Wacksman about their concerns, and Wacksman assured them that he would place conditions that would allow Duncan to visit only when he was being supervised. Wacksman explained to them that Duncan was a changed man.

"Obviously, he wasn't" said one of the neighbors.

—CHAPTER EIGHTEEN—

ALTHOUGH DUNCAN WAS CHARACTERIZED AS A BRIGHT individual, both as a youth and as an adult, he was "bored with school" and, due to excessive truancy, was failing nearly all of his classes at Lakes High School at the time he was expelled. Although he was fully capable of making good grades, he made mostly Cs, Ds and Fs the last two years that he was in school. As a child he was characterized as immature, and by the time he was sent to prison for the rape of the 14-year-old boy he did not seem to appreciate the seriousness of his situation. Instead, he was preoccupied with thoughts of his 14-year-old girlfriend, and believed that she would marry him when he obtained his release. Although the authorities had written up reports recommending that he be sentenced as an adult, he didn't seem overly concerned. Instead he talked about how he would rather be with kids his own age and go back to school. He had expressed an interest in scuba diving and sky diving, but had otherwise shown no initiative in applying himself academically. His grade point average dropped to an all-time low of 1.7 during this time. Duncan later told a pre-sentence investigator that he was smoking marijuana on a daily basis by the time he'd entered high school, and had tried

Brenda Groene and Mark McKenzie mug shots, taken after minor scrapes with the law in Idaho. *Kootenai County, Idaho Sheriff's Department*

Police artist rendering of suspect in kidnapping and sex slaying of Anthony Martinez, *left, courtesy Riverside County Sheriff's Department*, and mug shot of sex offender Joseph Edward Duncan III following his arrest in Coeur d'Alene, Idaho, for the kidnapping of Shasta Groene and the murder of her family, *courtesy Kootenai County Sheriff's Department.*

Missing Child poster issued by the Riverside County, California Sheriff's Department following the kidnapping of Anthony Martinez.

Leanna "Beaner" Warner, 5, disappeared from her Chisholm, Minnesota, home. Joseph Edward Duncan III was scrutinized as a potential suspect in her disappearance. *Courtesy Chisholm, Minnesota Police Department*

Half-sisters Carmen Cubias, 9, *left*, and Sammiejo White, 11, *right*, disappeared from a Seattle, Washington, motel in July 1996. Their remains were found two years later in Bothell, Washington, about 15 miles from Seattle. Joseph Edward Duncan III became a suspect in their deaths after talking to investigators in Idaho. *Bothell, Washington Police Department*

Hank Eisses, *left*, and Victor Vazquez, *right*, convicted sex offenders, were found slain on August 27, 2005, in the Bellingham, Washington, home they shared. Police later determined that Michael A. Mullen, 36, killed the two men after Mullen claimed to have been inspired to kill sex offenders after following Joseph Edward Duncan's case in Idaho. *Bellingham, Washington Police Department*

Sex offender Joseph Edward Duncan III, mug shot after arrest in Coeur d'Alene, Idaho. *Kootenai County Sheriff's Department*

An earlier mug shot of Joseph Edward Duncan III, undated. *Fargo, North Dakota Police Department*

Dylan Groene, 9, was murdered at a Montana campground. Investigators have accused Joseph Edward Duncan III of Dylan's slaying. *Associated Press*

Kootenai County Sheriff Rocky Watson as he prepares to tell reporters about the details of the triple homicide at the Groene-McKenzie residence. *Associated Press*

The house where Brenda and Slade Groene and Mark McKenzie were found murdered on May 25, 2005. Shasta Groene, 8, and her brother, Dylan, 9, were missing from the home. *Associated Press*

Police remove one of the three bodies found inside the Groene-McKenzie home near Wolf Lodge, just outside Coeur d'Alene, Idaho. *Associated Press*

Steve Groene and his daughter, Shasta, after being reunited following Shasta's rescue at Denny's Restaurant in Coeur d'Alene. *Associated Press*

A security video camera caught this image of Shasta Groene and her abductor, Joseph Edward Duncan III, in a Kellogg, Idaho, convenience store only hours before her rescue. *Associated Press*

Shasta Groene, 8, at the Kootenai Medical Center in
Coeur d'Alene following her rescue. *Associated Press*

Kootenai County Prosecuting Attorney Bill Douglas as he speaks to reporters following Joseph Edward Duncan's arraignment. *Associated Press*

Registered Sex Offender Joseph Edward Duncan III

Credits, left to right: Tacoma, Washington Police Department; Fargo, North Dakota Police Department; Kootenai County Sheriff's Department

LSD, amphetamines, barbiturates, valium and PCP (also known as angel dust).

Nonetheless, by the time he was actually released from prison he had obtained his GED and would later gain admittance to North Dakota State University, where he excelled in his studies in the field of computer software engineering. He made the dean's list in the fall 2000 and spring 2001 semesters, showing great promise in his field of endeavor.

According to his prison records, Duncan's family had moved around a lot, including overseas, due to his father's military career. Duncan admitted to acts of burglary and shoplifting, and told therapists and counselors that there had always been a lot of turmoil in his home and that his parents were often fighting with each other. He told a prison official in 1992 that he was relieved that his parents were no longer living together.

According to his mother, Duncan never had many friends while growing up. He regressed when his brother, Bruce, was born, and he wet the bed until he was 13 years old. He was known to go to school wearing dirty underwear and was teased by his peers. He always had a very bad temper, which he learned how to control later on in his prison life. His mother stated that he had a good personality, but erupted on occasion. She told a prison counselor that his problems might be related to the fact that he preferred to eat starches and sweets.

After his brother moved in with his father following their parents' separation, Duncan became very withdrawn and would spend much of his time alone in his bedroom, in a depressed state of mind. He would sleep all day but sneak out at night. According to his mother, he had high hopes of joining the Air Force—but those hopes were soon dashed when he was told that he had no chance of being accepted due to his past record. His mother said that he had little, if any, initiative and had a poor self-concept. He was always seeking everyone's approval, but rarely did anything to deserve it.

A number of the reports written by therapists and prison counselors clearly characterized Duncan as a sexual psychopath, a deviant who was not fit to be loose to roam the streets of any community.

"This position of power over children has developed into a very powerful and compulsive pattern," wrote clinical director Dr. William Voorhees Jr. "It is important to note that Mr. Duncan did go out looking for victims . . . He exhibited little remorse or guilt for his sexual deviation while in treatment . . . Mr. Duncan is not safe to be at large."

As the authorities, particularly the FBI, continued their probe into Duncan's background and possible victims, they looked at a number of cases involving missing or murdered children in areas where Duncan could be placed in close proximity. One such case was that of 12-year-old Steven Earl Kraft Jr., who went missing from Benton Harbor, Michigan, while walking his dogs between 7 and 8 P.M. on February 15, 2001, approximately seven months after Duncan moved to Fargo, North Dakota. Although Fargo was some 700 miles from Benton Harbor, it was noted that serial killers often do a lot of driving and travel great distances as they troll for their victims.

Another possible victim being looked at was Shawn Hornbeck, 11, who disappeared on October 6, 2002, from

Richwoods, Missouri, last seen at approximately 4:30 P.M. while riding his bicycle. Richwoods is about 200 miles east of Kansas City, and it was known that Duncan sometimes visited relatives in the Kansas City area.

A third victim being viewed by investigators as possibly being attributable to Duncan was Dalton Mesarchik, 7 years old, who was last seen on March 26, 2003, in the front yard of his home in Streator, Illinois. His body was found in a river the following day. Interestingly, the boy had been bludgeoned to death with a hammer.

One more potential victim of Duncan's was Leanna "Beaner" Warner, 5, who was last seen between 5 and 5:30 P.M. on Saturday, June 14, 2003, in Chisholm, Minnesota. Chisholm, the investigators noted, is roughly 200 miles due east from Fargo. The girl was described as wearing a dark blue sleeveless denim dress and was barefoot when she disappeared. She was described as being 3 feet tall with brown shoulder-length hair and brown eyes.

Investigators noted that Duncan had posted an entry on his Web log in January 2004 in which he wrote that he was attempting to determine where he was when Leanna disappeared because he believed that investigators would consider him a prime suspect.

"Just found out that a five year old girl went missing from Chisholm MN on June 14, 2003," Duncan wrote. "I did not even know until today that this happened."

Investigators checked his movements during the period in which Leanna disappeared and learned that he may have been in her area at that time.

"Duncan is certainly in the back of our minds," said Bob Heales, a private investigator involved in helping

Leanna's father, Chris Warner, and a dog handler from South Dakota in their search for the girl. "It appears that Duncan was in Crosby and Grand Rapids the week prior to when Leanna went missing, and in Duluth the week after. Chisholm is pretty much in the middle of that territory. But you don't want to get tunnel vision. If you focus [only] on this guy, and he didn't do it, then you might lose the trail of the one who did take her." Heales emphasized that a key objective in renewing the search for Leanna is to "get Leanna's picture out there again. She could be out there somewhere, alive. People need to recognize Beaner when she walks into a Denny's restaurant with somebody."

One thing that began to emerge as investigators studied Duncan's Web log is that he posted to it regularly, and consistently outlined many of his activities in a clear and concise manner. The cops wondered if he had perhaps used the blog as a means to try to set up alibis to help him mask his real activities. An example is a meeting that occurred with a gay man named "Jeff," with whom he supposedly had developed a relationship.

"I met Jeff, a 'salesman' the other day and will be having lunch with him on Saturday after he meets with some other colleagues for breakfast," Duncan wrote. "Should be interesting." That entry was made on January 8, 2004. Another entry, made on January 10, 2004, said: "The meeting with Jeff was a bust. I tried calling him at 12:30 and 1:00 but he did not answer."

Another entry, made on January 13, 2004, titled "Sex and Mayhem," said: "Someone told me yesterday that I was different than most other sex offenders because I was only 16 when I committed my crime and have never committed any other sex crimes since (or before). However, the same person said that adult offenders should be castrated and locked up for life." Another entry, nine days later, read: "I invited 'Jeff' . . . over for a quicky. He fucked me . . . and I loved it. He was only here for 20 minutes at the most. We are going to do it again Saturday."

In other entries he also listed dates, times and distances from Fargo to the locations where he supposedly had traveled. Investigators could only wonder why he had decided to be so detailed.

—CHAPTER NINETEEN—

ON INDEPENDENCE DAY WEEKEND, THE CAMERON CONOCO in Kellogg, Idaho, became the source of much police activity. As it turned out, an employee at the gas station had seen a man and a young girl who matched Duncan's and Shasta's description pull into the station in a red Jeep the day before Shasta was rescued in Coeur d'Alene. The man had filled up the Jeep with gas, and afterward he and the girl entered the food mart. It wasn't until they had come inside that they caught the station employee's attention.

"I thought, 'That girl looks like Shasta,'" the employee said later, after reporting the sighting. "She didn't seem nervous, mistreated, nothing out of the ordinary. I almost asked her name. I would've said, 'You look like this Shasta girl I know.' But I didn't, because I didn't know if she was with her father."

The employee figured that the man and the girl were not Shasta and Duncan until she saw the Jeep Duncan was driving on the news later. After she recognized the red Jeep, the employee called the station's manager and they viewed the store's video surveillance tapes together. After recognizing Duncan and Shasta, but not seeing Dylan, they notified the Kootenai County Sheriff's Department. The FBI promptly responded.

"I felt sick all day," the employee, a mother of three children, said. "I should have called [sooner]. They could have found her six hours earlier. It was really hard yesterday. Here she was with this creep longer than she should've been."

A short time later, news of Dylan began to emerge.

SHASTA AND DYLAN WERE REPEATEDLY MOLESTED," DEtective Brad Maskell wrote in an affidavit released on Tuesday, July 5, 2005. "Shasta saw Mr. Duncan molest Dylan." The intent of the crimes was to rape, seriously injure or to commit a lewd and lascivious act on a child under the age of 16, according to the public information that became available. Maskell also revealed publicly for the first time that a day earlier, on Independence Day, authorities had been led to two remote campsites in a logging area of western Montana, primarily by directions provided by Shasta, where human remains were found at one of the sites. He indicated that, pending positive identification, they believed the remains were those of 9-year-old Dylan Groene.

The site that Shasta had led investigators to was located in the Bitterroot mountains, just off of Interstate 90 near St. Regis, Montana. St. Regis is located approximately 100 miles east of Coeur d'Alene. According to U.S. Forest Service Officer Clint McGuffey, who was asked to help coordinate an effort to secure the suspected crime scenes, the campsites that were being searched were in the vicinity of Little Joe and Two Mile

Creeks. The site, like most of the remote areas in the 2.2-million-acre Lolo National Forest region, consists of a maze of heavily forested logging roads dotted with makeshift campsites. The FBI, the Kootenai County Sheriff's Department and the Mineral County, Montana, Sheriff's Department, which was assisting in the case, took one of the most remote roads in the area and followed it to its end. The road, about three and one-half miles long, was little more than a narrow trail barely wide enough for a vehicle to traverse. Shasta had apparently shown investigators an approximate location on the map, and said that she recalled that it was in the "Lolo" forest not too far off of the freeway.

At the end of the road, if it could be called a road, the investigators found a makeshift campsite. A trail had been cut through an alder thicket that led to and from a small fire ring, presumably left by Duncan where he and the children had camped. There were freshly cut branches in the area, and a large ponderosa pine tree from which sap oozed out of slits made with a knife and deeper cuts apparently made by an ax or hatchet.

Although Maskell would not confirm that the location was where the human remains were found and would only comment that investigators were "checking out a lot of different sites," a local officer from Mineral County confirmed to a reporter on condition of anonymity that this was the spot. It was found, the officer told the reporter, following a search that had taken most of the weekend. Investigators had utilized a topographic map of the area and had been able to pinpoint the location based on Shasta's recollections.

The remains were carefully gathered up from a nearby

culvert and bagged, and were being sent to the FBI's forensic laboratory in Quantico, Virginia. According to Sheriff Rocky Watson, it would take a minimum of seventy-two hours to complete DNA testing to determine whether the remains were, in fact, Dylan's. There was little doubt in anyone's mind at this point, however.

In the meantime, as news of the grisly discovery were slowly being made public, residents of St. Regis, a town of barely 100 residents, expressed shock and sadness that Shasta and Dylan had been in their midst and nobody had noticed. Posters of the two children had been placed at various locations in town shortly after the children disappeared.

"Everybody feels bad," said one St. Regis resident. "We may have been able to spot them. We've never seen anything like this."

A St. Regis service station and food mart manager came forward after she realized that Duncan had visited her store nearly a month earlier. He had filled up his vehicle with gas and purchased a 12-pack of Bud Light. He spoke with the store employee for about fifteen minutes, making mostly small talk, but occasionally asking her questions about the area's parks and campgrounds, as well as driving directions to other communities. The employee said that she was "shocked and stunned" when she learned that the man she'd seen was Duncan. She said that she had been on the lookout for Shasta and Dylan ever since they'd disappeared, just like other area residents who had been watching for suspicious activity among the tourists making their way toward Glacier National Park.

"I know people can fool you," she said, "but he was a

really clean-cut and relaxed guy. It just kind of shocked me. I still don't know what to think. . . . You hate for this kind of thing to happen anywhere, but especially for it to happen so close to home."

—CHAPTER TWENTY—

ON WEDNESDAY, JULY 6, 2005, INVESTIGATORS CLAIMED that they had positively linked Joseph Edward Duncan III to the slayings of Brenda and Slade Groene and Mark McKenzie. Although Captain Ben Wolfinger would not discuss specific evidence that tied Duncan to the brutal slayings (which likely would not be revealed until trial), Wolfinger stated that the investigators believed that Duncan had acted alone.

"There's a sense of relief that we have the right guy," Wolfinger said. According to Wolfinger, detectives now believed that Duncan had picked the family at random and that the slayings and subsequent kidnappings were the result of meticulous planning.

"It was not a spontaneous act," agreed Sheriff Rocky Watson. "I think they were likely randomly selected, though."

"At first the detectives believed the perpetrator was somebody known to the family," said Steve McKenzie. "Now, all sides of the family, everybody involved, can really grieve together and not be suspicious of who this person is. . . . Everybody had painted this picture of a crazy drug scene. It was never that way. . . . What a courageous little fighter Shasta is to go through so much and to still be able to smile and be happy to see people."

Sheriff Watson agreed that the investigators, himself included, had had a great deal of difficulty making any sense out of the crime scene because it had not fit neatly into any written profiles that he had read.

"When you walk into that type of violent crime scene," Watson said, "those things are usually driven by sex, money or drugs, and nothing fit. This incident is going to rewrite a chapter in profiling. It doesn't fit what we're used to. I've not seen anything and not read anything like this."

Although the investigators were not commenting publicly about a possible motive for the crimes that Duncan was accused of committing, there was plenty circulating among the area residents, as well as in the media, that Duncan's planning of the crimes was sexually motivated. The investigators said nothing to discount such theories.

"This guy has a history of tying people up and beating people," Jesse Groene said from the Shoshone County Jail in Wallace, Idaho, where he was serving time for burglary and grand theft charges. "That's what happened to my family. I have no doubt he's the one who murdered them. . . . If they don't give Duncan the death penalty, then I'm gonna . . ." He was overcome with emotion and couldn't finish the sentence.

That same day a reporter showed up at Duncan's mother's apartment in the Tacoma suburb of Lakewood, only a short distance from where she had lived with her family in the 1970s. When Lillian Mae Duncan answered the door, it was clear to the reporter that she was very distraught.

"I can't make any statements," she told the reporter, tears running down her face. "I just don't know what to do. I have some people that I need to call. I'm sorry."

A short time later, she hung a handwritten sign on her front door that read: "Do not disturb. Not available. Soliciting of any kind not permitted here."

Meanwhile, as news of Duncan's background began to seep into public view, curiosity surrounding his prior criminal history turned to outrage over the state of Washington's inability to keep him behind bars for life, despite its civil commitment law, which allowed the state to hold violent sexual predators indefinitely, even after they had completed their sentences. People demanded to know why Duncan had been let out.

Victoria Roberts, chairwoman of the state's End of Sentence Review Committee, said at a news conference that the crime for which Duncan had been convicted was two decades old by the time he was released in the year 2000. She claimed that there wasn't adequate information to indicate that Duncan remained a threat.

"The rape occurred when he was sixteen," Roberts said. "He was thirty-seven [when he was released], which is a huge difference developmentally. . . . There just wasn't enough evidence [to hold him beyond his sentence completion]."

Roberts told reporters that Duncan's case had been reviewed for possible civil commitment, and that an additional psychological evaluation had been done. The rape that Duncan committed, said Roberts, wasn't considered pedophilia because there was less than a five-year age difference between him and his victim, and Duncan later recanted all of the other rapes that he had claimed to have committed. According to Roberts, Duncan had made up the other rapes in order to get into a treatment program at a mental institution rather than being sent to prison.

"And twenty years later there was nothing to substantiate that those things [the recanted rapes] had occurred," Roberts said.

There was also no evidence that Duncan had re-offended during his period of freedom in Seattle.

"All of the bases were covered," Roberts said. "And given what we knew at the time, I think the right decision was made. . . . The dilemma is that when we're looking at sex offenders . . . and the offense is committed when the person is a juvenile, do we really want to begin locking these people up for the rest of their lives for something that they might do in the future?"

Steve Groene, among others, believes that whatever needs to be done to keep violent sex offenders off the streets should be done. He called on the public to begin letter-writing campaigns.

"People need to start complaining to their elected officials," Groene said, "and we need to get some laws changed, and we need to do it quickly. . . . This needs to stop here. People like this [Duncan] should not be out in public."

Groene's son, Jesse, believes that the current laws are too lax when it comes to violent sex offenders.

"People who can't control themselves sexually and conduct sexual crimes," Jesse Groene said, "should be castrated or not let back on the streets."

Or, he said, put a tracking chip on the violent ones so that law enforcement will always know where they are.

Polly Franks, a board member of the Coalition for Victims in Action, believes that the current sex offender registration laws lack "teeth," and is pushing for a national registry which, she believes, may help prevent crimes like those that have been attributed to Duncan.

"They've relied on the honor system for hardened sex offenders, which would be funny if it wasn't so terrible," Franks said.

Even though there are laws on the books of most states that require convicted sex offenders to register with their local law enforcement agency any time they move across town or relocate to another state, many of them fail to follow the rules, even though it is a felony when they fail to register.

"If you've got someone in a neighboring state who's convicted, and he moves across the street from you, you'll have no idea," Franks said. Franks said that her own two daughters were attacked by a neighbor and family friend who had been convicted of rape in another state. A nationwide registry, she believes, could help prevent such attacks—provided, of course, the offender has registered in the first place.

The case in northern Idaho, said Franks, "was a preventable tragedy." Franks pointed out that even though Duncan was categorized as one of the most high-risk sex offenders in Fargo, North Dakota, a judge in Minnesota had freed him when Duncan wrote a $15,000 bad check to make his bail after he had been charged with molesting a 6-year-old boy.

"When these Level IIIs are let go," she said, "we should not be surprised when the public suffers terribly."

Michael Paranzino, president of a group in Maryland

called Throw Away the Key, which encourages incarceration and civil commitment of violent sex offenders, expressed his outrage that someone like Duncan was released on bail in Minnesota.

"It is nearly useless to know that your own street or neighborhood has no molesters," Paranzino said, "because a bus, car or subway can put thousands of molesters within your child's reach within minutes. . . . This is a tragedy for one family, but a scandal for our justice system. Can you believe they had a violent, convicted child molester arrested for a new molestation and they let him out on bail?"

Detroit Lakes, Minnesota, attorney Stuart Kitzmann had stopped by the county courthouse on the morning of April 5, 2005, so that he could get a look at the man who had been accused of molesting the two young boys in broad daylight at the elementary school playground. Kitzmann was the only person in the courtroom gallery that morning, and he was surprised and angry when he heard the judge set Duncan's bail at $15,000. He became even more upset as he watched Duncan leave the courthouse after writing the court a personal check for his bail.

"He was walking down the sidewalk talking on his cell phone," Kitzmann said. "I saw him throw his head back, laughing. I was freaked out by the whole thing. It just disturbed me. I wanted to get out of my car and tackle the guy."

Many people began wondering whether or not the tragedies in northern Idaho would have occurred had Duncan's bail been set at an amount that would have made it more difficult for him to pay.

—CHAPTER TWENTY-ONE—

On Sunday, July 10, 2005, Kootenai County Sheriff's Captain Ben Wolfinger held a brief news conference in which he sadly announced that the remains found in the Bitterroot mountains west of St. Regis, Montana, were indeed those of 9-year-old Dylan Groene. Wolfinger refused to respond to questions, but confirmed that the FBI's DNA analysis of the remains was how the identification was made.

As the identification became public knowledge, rumors began circulating surrounding the manner of death that the child had endured at Duncan's hands, which authorities would neither confirm nor deny. Media reports were claiming that Dylan had been cremated. Other rumors said that Duncan had made videos of himself as he molested and raped the two children, which purportedly had begun soon after the homicides of Shasta and Dylan's family. The existence of at least one video had already been confirmed by Kootenai County authorities, and they'd already revealed Shasta's statement that Duncan had killed her brother with a shotgun.

There was also wild talk of how Duncan had made videotapes of Dylan hanging by his neck from a rope or cord, and that the video depicted the boy on the verge of death, only to be lifted up and revived—and when he had regained consciousness, the horrible ordeal began again. Another rumor was that Duncan had forced Shasta to drag her brother, half-dead from the hanging, by the rope around his neck through the campfire, videotaping the scene. Duncan then killed Dylan with a shotgun, and used a hatchet to chop up the little boy, after which he forced Shasta to place her brother's body parts into the fire—or so the rumors said. Sometime later, again according to rumor, Duncan videotaped Shasta as he forced her to pick her brother's burnt body parts out of the cooled-down campfire ashes, after which they were thrown into a culvert with the hope, presumably, that they would be washed away by the next heavy rainfall.

No one, of course, except the cops and Duncan, and possibly Shasta, knew for sure what had been done to the little boy. But the speculation was enough to keep the public stirred up for some time to come.

A short while later, however, an article appeared in the *Globe*, a weekly tabloid, which said that Shasta had been forced to watch while Duncan molested Dylan, burned him with cigarettes, and beat him with a stick before killing him. The *Globe* article attributed their information to Kootenai County Sheriff's Sergeant Brad Maskell. If the report turned out to be accurate, some of the details were chillingly similar to what Duncan had done to the 14-year-old Tacoma boy he had raped in the forest twenty-five years earlier.

Former FBI profiler Clint Van Zandt told the *Globe* that Duncan's crimes in northern Idaho and western Montana might be only the tip of the iceberg.

"Duncan may well be responsible for kidnaps and murders that have not been identified yet," Van Zandt said. "This guy didn't just fall off the turnip truck two months ago and decide that he is going to start killing. He got out of jail in 2000. There is a possibility that he has sexually molested other children and murdered other people, too."

Dr. Park Dietz, another criminal profiler who has worked on many cases of well-known but notorious serial killers like John Wayne Gacy, Jeffrey Dahmer, and others, agreed with Van Zandt.

"It is certainly possible that there are other bodies out there [attributable to Duncan]," Dietz said. "Obviously, he is a sexual predator, obviously a spree killer and obviously a mass murderer. And he may turn out to be a serial killer."

According to *Justice* magazine, police searches of the red Jeep that Duncan was driving when he was arrested turned up a video camera, a digital video recorder, memory cards, and a laptop computer, among other things. *Justice* was also able to confirm with multiple law enforcement sources that Duncan's digital image library included at least one recording of Dylan (it should be recalled that Kootenai County authorities had confirmed the existence of a videotape). *Justice* did not provide details of what the images consisted of, but they did run a quote, confirming the material's existence.

"It's true," said Mineral County, Montana, Prosecuting Attorney M. Shaun Donovan. "I haven't seen the tape personally and I'm not able to tell you anything about the details of it."

Another Mineral County official, who spoke to *Justice* magazine on the condition of anonymity, said that federal investigators would not even "discuss it because of what's involved. I just heard the word, 'bad.' "

Justice also confirmed that the cause of death listed on Dylan's death certificate was a shotgun wound.

Also lending credence that there was likely some substance to all of the rumors was a story by Steve Huff about the Duncan case that had appeared on CrimeLibrary.com. In that article Huff stated that Dylan had been "murdered, his remains burned, and dismembered."

Compounding all of the confusion surrounding what may or may not have happened to Dylan was a statement by Shasta's father in the local media. Steve Groene told reporters for the *Spokesman-Review* that Shasta had not known the fate of her brother until the family had received official notification from the authorities, despite statements by Kootenai County authorities that Shasta had told them Duncan had shot her brother.

"She asked me last week in the hospital if I knew what had happened to Dylan," Groene told reporters.

A grimly positive side to the news that the remains in Montana had been confirmed as Dylan's was that it brought some sense of closure to his family.

"Steve has some comfort in knowing where all his children are," said Wendy Price, Dylan and Shasta's aunt. "Every parent wants to be able to put their child to rest. In a situation like this, there has to be something to cling on to. We know that Dylan and Slade are with their mother now."

DUNCAN WAS CHARGED WITH FOUR COUNTS OF FIRST-degree murder, in addition to several counts of kidnapping under various theories of law. Kootenai County

Prosecutor Bill Douglas said that his office would be seeking the death penalty against Duncan. Duncan pleaded innocent to the charges.

Adding still more credibility to the rumors about the manner of Dylan's death and the existence and content of the videotape(s) was the fact that, according to U.S. Attorney Tom Moss of the Boise, Idaho, office, federal authorities were going to wait until after the state of Idaho completed its case against Duncan before charging him in federal court with kidnapping Shasta and Dylan, transporting the minor children across state lines and killing Dylan, and possibly with other crimes.

"Besides the kidnapping charges, we don't know for sure what else we will file," said Jean McNeil, a spokesperson for the U.S. Attorney's Office. "There are various possibilities, and one is child pornography." McNeil said that there existed "various pieces of evidence" to support child pornography charges, but she declined to be more specific.

—CHAPTER TWENTY-TWO—

IN AN INTERESTING TURN OF EVENTS AS REPORTED BY MSNBC, two female college students who'd lived in downtown Fargo, North Dakota, two years before had filed a complaint with the Fargo police against Joseph Edward Duncan III. The two roommates had been frightened by Duncan because he had been exhibiting what they considered to be unusual behavior and loitering in the parking lot of their apartment building. They said that he had also hidden in the bushes outside. Neither of the two realized that Duncan was a sex offender until later, when one of them checked a local sex offender website and recognized Duncan's mug shot. Police felt at the time that the evidence was not strong enough to warrant bringing charges. One of the women, Megan Fisher, had accused Duncan of stalking, and she reported how frightened she had been of Duncan—so much so that on one occasion she had asked her father, attorney Dennis Fisher, to come over to the apartment. Two years later, after confronting Duncan and telling him to stop hanging around the building where his daughter lived, Fisher represented Duncan on the child molestation charge in Becker County, in which Duncan had jumped bail just prior to going to Idaho. Fisher told a local television station that he had not realized until later that Duncan was the same man his daughter had accused of stalking her and her roommate.

Duncan apparently wrote about the aforementioned situation on his Web log. He of course denied any involvement and complained that the women had accused him of harassment. One of the roommates said that she had been "creeped out" by the fact that Duncan had written about them, and expressed feelings of guilt that she could not have done more at the time to get Duncan back behind bars where he belonged.

"Not that it's my fault [that Duncan did what he did in Idaho]," said the young woman. "I do feel that guilt that all this has happened and I shrugged my shoulders and said, 'Nothing else will come of this.' "

Meanwhile, the subject of the videotape(s) that Duncan had allegedly made showing him with Shasta and Dylan continued to be an issue. The *Pacific Northwest Inlander*, a free weekly paper published in Spokane, reported that unidentified sources had said that cameras and tapes recovered from the stolen Jeep that Duncan had been driving contained footage of him abusing and threatening to kill the two children. The *Inlander* also reported that Duncan had photographed Dylan being shot to death. The footage appeared to depict the remote Montana campsite near where Dylan's remains were recovered. Citing unnamed sources who were working on the case, the *Inlander* reported that Duncan had filmed several attempts to kill the children, but that he had aborted the attempts when a gesture or action by either

Shasta or Dylan would cause him to stop videotaping. On one occasion, the *Inlander* said, Duncan didn't go through with an attempt to kill Dylan when, gagged and bound and only able to move his hands, the boy had made gestures to Shasta.

There was also a report that some of the footage may have made its way onto the Internet, perhaps placed there by Duncan himself before his capture. Kootenai County Prosecutor Bill Douglas was doing everything within his power to protect the videotapes, even to the extent that he said that he would not support making copies of them for Duncan's defense attorneys. Douglas also had the contents of the cameras encrypted to prevent unauthorized viewing, and told Duncan's attorneys that they had to come to his office if they wanted to see the tapes. Douglas said that he was being so protective of the photos and footage because they were too "sensitive, graphic, disturbing and offensive."

"We're asking the court to consider a couple of other reasons why we feel the state does not have to provide copies because of their sensitive nature," Douglas argued. Douglas said that he was concerned about the possibility of "inadvertent or accidental dissemination" of the videos, and said that his office would propose additional ways to accommodate Duncan's attorneys without making copies or compromising the investigation.

Douglas stated in court that he was concerned specifically about two video clips, each approximately ten to fifteen minutes long. He argued that the defense team had seen all of the videos and still photos that had been seized.

Duncan's public defender, John Adams, was naturally upset by the apparent leaks to reporters and by Douglas's attempts to keep the digital images out of the defense team's hands. Adams countered by saying that he was not convinced that the defense had seen everything there was to see, and that he had been told that there were as many as fifteen videos and hundreds of photographs. He said that Idaho State Police "related seeing numerous sex videos." Some of the videos, he said, may have already made their way into public view.

"We have a source inside of law enforcement that told us that he had been told some of those videos have made their way to the Internet," Adams said.

"All I can say is, the matter is the subject of an ongoing investigation," Douglas said. "I can't attest to the validity of those statements, whether they were made or not. . . . We maintain that they [the defense] have a lot of this stuff, or a lot of this stuff doesn't exist," he said, referring to a list of items compiled by the public defender's office.

"I thought this was a civilized society and Coeur d'Alene was a city of human rights, and not mob rule and trial by press and anonymous sources," Adams argued. "The state is really arguing that it is unwilling to make and provide copies of this material to the defense. Absent the discovery requested, Duncan will be deprived of his rights to the effective assistance of counsel both in preparation of and in presenting a defense."

First District Judge Fred Gibler sided with the defense and ordered the prosecutor to release the videos to Duncan's lawyers. Gibler said that he would set forth strict guidelines that would prevent the release of the videos to anyone other than the defense attorneys.

Meanwhile, it was publicly announced that Duncan had been ruled out as a suspect in the disappearance more than two years ago of 5-year-old Leanna "Beaner" Warner.

"Based on investigative results pertaining to where Duncan was on the day Leanna disappeared," said Chisholm, Minnesota, Police Chief Scott Erickson, "it has been determined that he is not a viable suspect in our case."

Leanna's father, Chris Warner, expressed both relief and disappointment over the announcement.

"It's a relief to know that an animal like that probably wasn't involved in her disappearance," Warner said. "But on the flip side, it kind of puts us back to square one."

Private investigator Bob Heales, who had been active in the search efforts to find Leanna, said that the news about Duncan no longer being a suspect would not deter him, and that it had prompted him to renew the search efforts. He said that he would be focusing on remote camping areas and forests in northern Minnesota that are similar to the location where Dylan's remains were found.

"We're glad to know one way or another," Heales said. "But it doesn't change the focus of what we're doing. We need to look in these areas no matter who was involved."

On Saturday, July 16, 2005, more than 700 people filed into a Coeur d'Alene church to remember Dylan Groene in a memorial service on what would have been his 10th birthday. Dylan was depicted by his friends and relatives as a kid who loved to play video games and to go motorcycle riding with his father.

Among the 700 mourners who attended the memorial service for Dylan at Real Life Ministries in Post Falls were friends, family members, teachers, law enforcement officers, bikers, and members of the community who wanted to pay their last respects to the slain child. Overhead a loud thunderstorm rumbled inside the large auditorium.

"I think you got a sense today, in person, about how God feels about this situation," Pastor Jim Putman told the somber, often tearful crowd. "I believe he wept for you to see his heart today."

At one point a video that depicted Dylan's life was played for the mourners. It consisted of photographs that had been taken at various stages of the boy's life: Dylan as a newborn, a kindergartner wearing a red Santa Claus hat, with his father sitting atop a Harley Davidson motorcycle, and one of Dylan, Shasta and Slade sitting on the tailgate of a pickup during a family outing.

Many local law enforcement officers as well as FBI agents attended the service. Idaho State Police Captain Wayne Longo was asked later if there were many tears shed during the investigation.

"Actually, a lot of us have shed a lot of tears over the eight weeks we've been working this," Longo said. "It's been a roller coaster of emotions. You feel so vulnerable."

Many teachers from Fernan Elementary School, which Dylan and Shasta had attended since kindergarten, were in attendance, as was the school's principal.

"The kids become one of yours," said Tim Marks, 35,

Dylan's third-grade teacher during the prior school year.
"You're losing somebody who's close to you."

"We love him and we'll miss him," said Lana Hamilton, the principal of the elementary school he had attended in Coeur d'Alene.

"God takes care of evil, and I can trust him to do it," said Pastor Jim Putman in an obvious reference to Duncan. "When he punishes, he does it far better than I could ever do."

A readerboard sign at Davis Donuts in Coeur d'Alene expressed things in a different way: "Duncan, Welcome to Idaho, a death penalty state. May you get your wish and die."

—CHAPTER TWENTY-THREE—

MOST PEOPLE IN COEUR D'ALENE BELIEVED THAT DUN-can should receive a sentence of execution if found guilty—and some said that his punishment should go beyond the death penalty. The few who thought his life should be spared believed that he nonetheless deserved horrific punishment of some sort.

"He needs to be castrated and thrown in a cave," said one area resident. "When there's that much evidence, he deserves to die. I don't think the standard execution is enough."

Even the pastor of St. Lukes Episcopal Church, the Reverend Patrick W. Bell, who did not normally believe in the death penalty, expressed his opinion outside of church that Duncan should die for his crimes.

"How can you do this to kids and even the parents?" Bell asked. "At what point do you finally say, 'Maybe it's time something has to change'? Even though we have finally talked about it here with our staff, it took us weeks to even mention it. It's so awful that it's almost like we can't talk about it."

"I think he has done so much hurt and so much damage for so many people," said an area business owner who was among those advocating the death penalty for Duncan.

One of the elements that made the case so chilling and upsetting to Coeur d'Alene residents was the fact that Duncan had selected the Groene house in Wolf Lodge Bay at random and then watched it and its residents for days, even utilizing night-vision goggles to peer inside their windows at night before deciding to carry out the acts of senseless violence.

"It was so premeditated and it was such a horrific, heinous crime, I don't see how he couldn't get the death penalty," said a local citizen.

"I think a lot of people in this town are very angry," said another resident. "They're mad as hell. Coeur d'Alene isn't used to this. This isn't southern California, it's Coeur d'Alene, and things like that aren't supposed to happen here."

Tom Keefe, former chairman of the Spokane County Democratic Party and a former candidate for Congress said that he is normally "pretty soft" when it comes to the death penalty, except when it applies to Joe Duncan.

"It's a very human response that the first thing we want to do is remove this vermin from the face of the earth," Keefe said. "This guy is an easy, charismatic candidate for the death penalty. . . . There are certain types of behavior that I don't think are able to be changed by a penal system or by education. What do you do with time bombs? If there's a case left for the death penalty in the state of Idaho, I'm sure a lot of people would say this guy would win the election."

Even Duncan's younger brother, Bruce Duncan, 40,

believed that his brother should be executed if found guilty of the crimes of which he'd been accused.

"They should fry his ass," Bruce told the *National Enquirer*. "Don't let him do this to another family. Keep him locked up or whatever the penalty is—just put him away. . . . He should still be in prison for raping a fourteen-year-old boy at gunpoint . . . the one thing that could have prevented what happened in Idaho is to have never let him out.

"Joe thought," Bruce continued, " 'If I'm going back to prison, I'm going to go back big.' He felt he wasn't in control of his own life, so he had to control someone else's. He also had a twisted desire for children. He wanted to strike back at society, which he felt had done him wrong."

According to what Bruce told the *Enquirer*, his brother had not always been a monster. He explained that he and Joe had had a normal childhood, and that Joe was a quiet child who spent a lot of his spare time fantasizing. He liked to put on a cape and pretend that he was Superman. He also learned how to be manipulative at an early age.

"He knew how to cry on command when we were disciplined by our mother," Bruce said. "He would start crying and our mom would let up on him. From an early age he was a manipulator."

Bruce said that both he and Joe had been Boy Scouts, and it was after joining a local scouting group that Duncan may have had his first sexual experience with another boy. He recalled how Joe had stolen a car, tried to outrun the cops and crashed through a roadblock, resulting in injuries to his face that had required reconstructive surgery. "That's when everything started going downhill," Bruce said.

Bruce said that he was shocked when he learned that his brother had become a cross-dresser. "He said he had a black girlfriend who used to help him cross-dress and apply make-up," Bruce said. "They also had a sexual relationship. But for the most part he had relations with men. If you take a kid at sixteen years old and put him in prison with hardened criminals, you'll end up with a monster, and then you turn that monster loose on the streets . . . He didn't reform—he got out looking at people as prey."

Bruce explained that he had trouble believing that Shasta had been found alive with his brother.

"I just cried," he said. "Not for my brother, but for that family. I can't believe my own blood brother did this."

—CHAPTER TWENTY-FOUR—

Early on Saturday morning, August 27, 2005, at 3:08 a.m. and nearly 400 miles west of Coeur d'Alene, the Bellingham, Washington, Police Department received a telephone call from a man named James Russell, 42. Russell had just returned home from work and was frantic after finding his roommate, Hank Eisses, 49, lying on the carpet in a bedroom. Russell could see blood and he assumed that Hank was seriously injured. Russell, scared, left the house, located at 2825 Northwest Avenue, and called 911 from a nearby location where he waited for officers to arrive.

The responding officers soon met with Russell and a short time later entered the one-story home, where they found Eisses in the northwest bedroom with dried blood on his head and scalp. Blood was also pooling under his head. It was apparent that he was dead. Moments later, officers found a second body, another male, a few feet away in the same bedroom near a computer that was running. He was also dead, and was later identified as Victor Vasquez, 68.

The Whatcom County Medical Examiner's Office later determined the cause of death of each of the dead men. Eisses had died of a single gunshot wound that had entered his skull near his right earlobe and exited his left cheek. The force of the impact had caused a cranial fracture. Victor Vasquez also died as a result of a single gunshot wound. Evidence showed that the weapon had been in contact with Vasquez's right temple when it was fired, and the round had exited through his left eye.

During a subsequent search of the bedroom, two spent 9mm casings were recovered. The investigating officers noted that the computer monitor near Vasquez's body was in the ON position and was displaying a Whatcom County website for Level III sex offenders. A forensic examination of the computer showed that information on three Level III offenders—both Eisses and Vasquez, along with a third man—and an adult pornography site had been accessed between 9:30 and 10 P.M. the previous evening.

Vasquez, investigators learned, had been convicted in 1991 of molesting several relatives. His victims had suffered regular abuse, sexual and otherwise, according to official records. He had been released from prison about two years earlier, and was under Department of Corrections supervision at the time of his murder.

Eisses, they learned, had been sentenced to 5½ years in prison in 1997 for raping a 13-year-old boy at his home in Sumas, Washington, located near the Canadian border. Kathryn Bail, corrections department field supervisor for Whatcom County, told the detectives that Eisses had been released from department supervision approximately two years earlier.

When detectives interviewed Russell, the surviving roommate, they were told that a man had come to the house at approximately 7 P.M. on Friday, August 26. The man had claimed to be an off-duty FBI agent who had stopped to warn the three roommates that there was a "hit list" that had been issued for Level III sex offenders. All of the roommates were on the registry. The "FBI agent" claimed that two offenders had already been killed, and the matter was currently being investigated.

According to Russell's statement, the man was wearing a dark baseball cap with "FBI" printed on it. He was also wearing a dark-colored warm-up–type suit with white stripes down the sides and had a tattoo on his leg that appeared to be made up of two letters. He asked Russell for some beer, but Russell told him that he did not have any in the house and that he did not drink.

The FBI man then used a cellular telephone to make a call, and a short time later a van arrived. He left for a few minutes and returned with a "half-rack" of Coors beer. It appeared to Russell that the van was driven by a woman. The "FBI agent" told Russell "not to worry, because it was his partner." The vehicle left again and the man drank and smoked Camel cigarettes with Russell, Eisses and Vasquez outside the house while sitting in lawn chairs. The man knew Eisses's and Vasquez's names and backgrounds. He asked them to describe their offense histories and they complied. He then used his cell phone, presumably to check up on them, and assured them that he would get their classifications reduced in order to help protect them.

A short time later, Russell left the house to go to the bank before reporting to his job at 10 P.M. However, Russell had forgotten his wallet and returned home at approximately 9:30 to retrieve it and to see if the agent was still at the house. Entering through a side door, he ran into the FBI man. Russell told him that he had forgotten his wallet, and quickly went downstairs to his room. The FBI man told him, "Don't ever leave your wallet here again." Russell told the detectives that he hadn't seen or heard either of his roommates in or around the house. He then left and reported to work.

Russell said that he'd called home at about 1:15 A.M. to speak to Vasquez, but there was no answer. He said that it was unlike Vasquez not to answer the phone, because he was almost always up late working on his computers. At about 3 A.M., still unable to contact anyone at the house, Russell decided to drive home during his lunch break. When he arrived, he found the side door standing open and the hall light on. He told the detectives it was then that he discovered the first body.

The detectives asked Russell to show them any items that the FBI man might have touched or handled while he was at the house. Russell pointed out the lawn chairs, a beer can that had been discarded by the man and some of his cigarette butts.

Although by now the detectives figured that the murders were the work of a vigilante bent on ridding the world of sex offenders, they nonetheless fanned out and canvassed the neighborhood. They soon located a neighbor who recalled the man who had been at the sex offenders' home, talking in a loud voice. The neighbor provided the same basic description to the cops that Russell had provided, and added that he believed that the man was well over 6 feet tall. The neighbor told the cops that the man had gotten his attention because of his loud talking. The neighbor was aware that all three residents were Level III sex offenders, and said that he could hear the man talking about their status and making comments about the court system. The neighbor said that he had seen the FBI man throw one of his beer cans into the yard, and he remembered that small detail because the residents had always kept their yard neat and clean—the man's actions had not fit the way the house and yard were maintained.

The neighbor told the detectives that he later heard what he thought were either firecrackers or gunshots coming from the direction of the house that the FBI man was visiting. This had occurred sometime between 9:10 and 9:30 P.M. Soon after hearing the noises, he observed vehicle lights, and when he looked outside he saw a van pulling away from the driveway. Another neighbor also reported hearing what she believed were gunshots coming from the direction of the victims' house between 9:30 and 10:00 P.M.

As they made their way through the neighborhood, investigators soon located the store where the FBI man had purchased the beer. The store clerk recalled seeing the man, and was able to provide the detectives with his description. She recalled that he had paid with cash and believed that he had purchased the beer sometime between 7:40 and 8:00 P.M.

—CHAPTER TWENTY-FIVE—

ON WEDNESDAY, AUGUST 31, 2005, A REPRESENTATIVE OF the local media contacted the Bellingham Police Department with information about a letter that had been received from a person claiming responsibility for the sex offender murders. The letter writer stated that it was the dead men's status as Level III sex offenders that had motivated him to commit the killings, and he promised that there would be more murders to follow.

Forensic examination of the crime scene revealed a full DNA profile, as well as a partial fingerprint from one of the beer cans. Crime-scene analysts assured the detectives that identification could be made if a "known" sample or print was on file. The Washington State Crime Laboratory confirmed that a suspect's left thumb print had been recovered from one of the beer cans at the scene, and that laboratory examination of the spent shell casings showed that they were likely fired from a 9mm Smith & Wesson semiautomatic. There were no prints on either of the shell casings.

At approximately 7 P.M. on Monday, September 5, 2005, a 36-year-old man who identified himself as Michael A. Mullen called the Bellingham Police Department and said that he wanted to turn himself in for the murders of Hank Eisses and Victor Vasquez.

When Mullen was brought in to be interviewed by the detectives assigned to the case, he was advised of his constitutional rights, which he agreed to waive. The detectives then interviewed Mullen about his background and his knowledge of the murders. He explained that he had shot each of the victims in the head with a single round from a 9mm Smith & Wesson semiautomatic that he had stolen from a friend. He also said that he was guilty and that he wanted to receive the death penalty.

Mullen told the detectives that he was the letter writer as well, and asked if investigators had found his fingerprints on the Coors cans. He explained that he had brought gloves with him to the house but had forgotten to put them on. He then challenged the detectives to find his fingerprints on the shell casings, and explained that he had placed "gun oil" on them. Mullen said that he had been planning the crime for some time, and that he had researched the victims on the Internet as early as July 13. He told the cops things that only the killer would know, such as how he had the victims confirm their identities and describe their offenses before he killed them. He also told them how the bedroom computer had been used to log onto the Whatcom County sex offender website.

Mullen described himself as a thief and a "con" whose life had been wasted. He implied that murdering sex offenders had given his life value. He also said that he had been a victim of sexual abuse himself, although he never reported it at the time to either his family or to the authorities. He said that the recent child murders in

Idaho committed by Joseph Edward Duncan III had been a motivating factor in his actions, because "something had to be done." He said that he did not believe that the sex offender registration and notification system was working, and that sex offenders should be kept in prison for longer periods of time than they were currently. Mullen said that no one else was involved in the killings, but he was adamant that there were several others who would take up his work after he was sent to prison.

He claimed that the computer he had used for research and letter writing was one that he had rented at a Kinko's on Everett Mall Way in Everett, Washington. He said that he had taken a ferry to Orcas Island where he'd dumped the gun into Puget Sound.

The detectives eventually located and interviewed Mullen's acquaintances and family members, which eventually led them to a female with whom he had been staying both before and after the murders. Detectives asked the friend if she had a firearm, and she told them that she owned a 9mm Smith & Wesson semiautomatic. She also told them that she had recently discovered that it was missing and that it had been replaced with a pellet gun in the lockbox where she normally kept it. Notes from "Michael" were also found on electronic media inside her house. One of the notes read:

> You are going to be seeing and hearing a lot of things about me on the News, and some of it may be true; however, much of it will be media hype! Don't get me wrong, Murder is not a solution, and what I did was also wrong. However I can only pray that God will see my intentions were good. . . . I'm sorry I could not tell you of my inten-

tions. I have used you to accomplish my mission. Don't be too fooled, after all I have fooled the entire world, and this includes those I have been very close to. And when you notice that the gun is missing and has been replaced by a pellet gun, rest assured that "not" [sic] your gun that I used to carry out my acts. In fact your gun I threw into the Pudget [sic] Sound shortly after we got it out of the pawn shop. I was afraid with all the kids we had in the house . . .

As the investigators continued to talk with Mullen's friend about the murders, she began to realize that she had unknowingly provided Mullen with assistance in carrying out his crimes. He had earlier told the police that he had been staying in motels around the time of the murders and shortly thereafter. He had also told the police that he had taken taxis to and from the murder scene. His friend, however, told the police that Mullen had been staying with her.

On the day of the murders, she said, she had taken Mullen to Bellingham so that he could check on a possible rental on Northwest Avenue. She estimated that this had been on Friday evening, August 26. She said that she had dropped Mullen off at the house in her van and that he had told her not to come in but to visit a relative instead until he called her on his cell phone. He called a short time afterward, and she picked him up and took him to a store where he bought the beer. She then drove him back to the house, and left again. Later that evening he called her and instructed her to pick him up. She drove to the house and, following his instructions, waited for him in the driveway. However, a short time later she received another call in which Mullen told her that he was on the street a short distance from the house. She said that she then located him, picked him up and drove him home.

Mullen's friend gave the detectives permission to process her van as well as her computer for evidence. Letters that were connected with the case were found on her computer. A crushed Coors can was also found in a bag inside the van, and what appeared to be a blood smear was found on the passenger interior molding. She gave the investigators Mullen's cell phone number, and it was discovered from records for the land line into the victims' residence that Mullen had called the home at 4:10 P.M. on the day of the murders.

MULLEN'S BROTHER, LARRY, DESCRIBED MICHAEL AS someone who had lived a life of disappointment and crime, fear and betrayal, and had "been crying out for help all of his life," in part because of repeated victimization. Michael had said that he was molested by a neighbor when he was in the second or third grade, but the incident was never reported to the police. Michael never told anyone about it until years later.

"There were all the telltale signs" that the abuse had occurred, said Larry. He told the *Seattle Times* that there were four children in the family, and because of the fact that their parents worked so much, the children had had to "fend for themselves."

Michael had been a bed-wetter, and he'd seemed to struggle with the purported molestation. He'd dropped out of school in the eighth grade and begun drinking. He'd joined the Job Corps at one point, and was taken to Florida by one of the men running the program, where he was abandoned. Larry doesn't know much about what occurred in Florida, but he believes his brother may have been victimized again there.

"He was just a sweet kid," Larry said. "I just wish I had an answer."

At one point Michael became a con man, and in 1993 he was convicted after he passed a bad check for 150 pounds of veal from an Everett meat supplier. In 1997 he was convicted of theft in another scam, and he ended up doing two stretches in Washington prisons. He went through two marriages and fathered two children, all the while continuing his struggle with alcohol and, eventually, prescription drugs that included Xanax and sleeping pills.

At one point, Michael moved to California and bought a car from friends. However, he fell behind in his payments and left with the car without telling them, prompting them to eventually report it as stolen. He was convicted of vehicle theft in 2003 and spent 18 months in a California prison, "thrown into a cluster of real bad people," Larry said. "He saw people murdered in there. He saw people being raped . . . Something happened to him inside that California prison."

MULLEN, IN THE MEANTIME, WAS PORTRAYED AS AN avenging angel for child sex-crime victims, and was hailed as a hero on the Web after being charged with two counts of aggravated first-degree murder in the deaths of Eisses and Vasquez. Mullen, thinking that he would be put to death by the state, wrote to the *Seattle Times* and said that he welcomed the death penalty so that he could beat Duncan into the afterlife and hold him accountable for what he'd done in Idaho.

"I will see to it personally that their deaths and abuse was not in vain!" Mullen wrote.

Instead of facing the death penalty, however, Mullen reached a plea agreement in which he was allowed to plead guilty to two counts of second-degree murder.

"You put yourself above the law," said Whatcom County Superior Court Judge Ira Uhrig, "and by doing so, in some sense you put yourself above the rights of every citizen in the state of Washington."

Mullen wrote that "out of the three [sex offenders] only one [Russell] showed remorse or guilt. He is the one I let go . . . I came to the conclusion that they must die, along with my own execution at the hands of the state, to drive my point home that 'WE' will protect 'our' children."

Vasquez's daughter cried in the courtroom at Mullen's sentencing as she addressed her father's killer in open court, stating that Mullen had deprived her of being able to continue the renewed relationship that she had begun to develop with her father.

"He's dead and he's not supposed to be dead," she told Mullen.

After Mullen was sentenced to 44 years in prison as a result of his plea agreement, Vasquez's daughter told reporters that she was "absolutely satisfied. Now I can take time to grieve and mourn my loss."

—CHAPTER TWENTY-SIX—

AS THE NEW YEAR CAME AND WENT AND JOSEPH EDWARD Duncan III won trial delay after trial delay, Shasta Groene, now 9 years old and the sole survivor of the bloody rampage that had occurred at her home nearly a year ago, was still working at putting her life back together. From all appearances, one would say that she was doing a magnificent job of it, considering everything that she had been through. However, the emotional scars that lie beneath the outer veneer will be with her for a lifetime.

On Wednesday, March 29, 2006, Shasta returned to the house where her family had been murdered. She was there to help celebrate what would have been her brother Slade's 14th birthday. During an interview with a local television station, Shasta spoke in a normal voice for a child her age as she and other family members prepared to release balloons in a birthday tribute to Slade. The event marked the first time that Shasta had made a public comment since her rescue last July 2.

"I'm happy to be here and happy to be doing this," Shasta told KREM, a Spokane television station. "Slade's my brother and I want to do this for him."

She said that she had written a note to Slade, one to her mother, another to Dylan and one to Mark.

"Happy birthday," Shasta said. "And tell Mom and Dylan and Mark I love them and stuff. Hopefully we'll get to see them again."

Shasta said that her former home was special to her because she and her family had spent so much time there together.

"All of the kids pretty much grew up here," she said. "Our main bedtime was usually at eight thirty. If it was not a school night, she [her mother] would let us stay up longer."

Shasta characterized Slade as "a very nice boy, and we don't want to forget about him. We should pray for him every night . . . every holiday I would want him to be involved in the holidays, even though he is not here. That doesn't mean that he doesn't exist . . . In Christmas I would buy him a Christmas present. He was a really good brother to me and really sweet to people, and we all love him."

Shasta made no mention of Duncan during her televised interview.

DUNCAN'S LAWYER, JOHN ADAMS, SAID THAT HE WAS TRYing to negotiate a plea bargain that would spare Duncan the death penalty. Adams cautioned that if a deal was not reached, Shasta might have to testify repeatedly against Duncan for the next twenty years as he made appeal after appeal, particularly if he won any retrials based on appeals—assuming, of course, that he would be convicted.

"Take the death penalty out of the picture and I'm

sure the case will be over," Adams said. "It's unethical for a lawyer to plead his client to the death penalty. As long as that's there, the defense can't do anything."

Prosecutor Bill Douglas, however, said that he will continue his pursuit of the death penalty for Duncan.

AUTHORITIES LEARNED THAT JOSEPH EDWARD DUNCAN III was continuing his efforts at blogging while behind bars. According to an Associated Press news report, his messages were written and sent to a person on the outside who posted them on the Internet on Duncan's behalf. The person responsible wanted to remain anonymous, and said that she had been assisting him since November 2005 because she hoped that his continued writing might reveal something that would incriminate him in the offenses with which he has been charged. Much of what was attributed to Duncan was religious in nature, and written in longhand.

An FBI agent told AP, on condition of anonymity, that the agency had been unable to confirm conclusively that the messages were written by Duncan, but that agents had continued to monitor the blog posts under the assumption that the writings were Duncan's.

"There is a real dearth of information about him, anyway," said the agent. "We are certainly going to look at any of his writings, to see if they have any investigative value . . . I want him to write as much as he can."

According to Captain Ben Wolfinger, jailers at the Kootenai County jail could not confirm that the letters being posted on the blog had been coming from Duncan.

"We just don't know," Wolfinger said, despite the fact that all mail sent by inmates is read by jailers. "All we scan for are contraband requests or escape plans or plans to commit crimes. The rest of it just goes on through."

One such posting that was inconclusively being attributed to Duncan read:

> The "light" is the *truth*—God's truth. I "came into the light" (faced up to the truth of what I was doing) by bringing that little girl home. It was the hardest thing I ever had to do! Compared to "facing the light"—dying will be easy!

Hannah McFarland, a handwriting expert from Seattle, examined copies of the letters attributed to Duncan, which were provided to her by a Spokane television station. She compared the copies, which consisted of faxes and files obtained off the Internet, with documents known to be written by Duncan, and said that they appeared to have been written by the same person.

"It's a qualified opinion, because I didn't have original documents," McFarland said.

One of the more recent postings, titled "Blogging the Fifth Nail: Revelations," was dated Monday, January 23, 2006, and had a headline that read: "We Need Tougher Sex Crimes (Uh, . . . laws)." In the entry the writer, presumably Duncan, compared the nation's preoccupation with sex crimes and sex offenders with the failure of Prohibition in the 1920s, which, the writer claimed, caused organized crime to grow.

"So now we need to get 'tough on sex crimes?'" the entry read. "That's synonymous to saying, 'We need more sex crime!'"

The writer went on to state that sex offenders who come under greater scrutiny due to new laws being enacted will be incited to commit even more crimes to prove to the public and to the authorities that they still have control of their own lives.

"A very good friend of mine who happens to be a 'serial killer' told me that he committed more sex crimes during the two years he was on parole (including killing three children) than he did in the entire five years he was not on parole," declared the writer, who also stated that his friend the serial killer had not committed additional crimes until the police performed quarterly residence checks. "So now more people are dead and hurting because some police chief decided to take it upon himself to 'get tough on sex crime' . . ."

Who was Duncan's serial killer "friend?" Could he have been referring to himself?

—CHAPTER TWENTY-SEVEN—

THE TRAGIC TURN OF EVENTS IN NORTHERN IDAHO DURing the spring and summer of 2005, as well as the consequent aftermath, has caused many people to question the effectiveness of Megan's Law and to conclude that it does not adequately define how individual states should release sex offender information to the public. The issue was brought to the forefront by a video depicting Joseph Duncan with his alleged victim right beside him, captured by surveillance cameras at a convenience store and released to the public shortly after Shasta Groene's rescue. Because of the magnitude of the case, parents across the country and in Canada began wondering whether the current sex offender registry laws go far enough, not to mention whether they really work or not. Megan's Law was set up to require that all fifty states release information about sex offenders to the public, but it fell short of its mark because it did not define how the states would accomplish such a feat. Every state carries out the law in its own way, with some states mandating active notification where law enforcement personnel put up posters or go door-to-door and tell locals that there's a sex offender living in their midst. Twenty-two of the states, however, only require passive notification, which means that the residents themselves have to take the initiative to find out if a sex offender lives in their neighborhood or not. Passive notification requires residents to research the registries via the Internet or to write to their local law enforcement agencies. The bottom line, however, is that the system has to rely on the offenders themselves to register in an honor system that many of them do not obey.

"We are expecting them to go and visit their parole officers so that we can be informed of their presence in the community," said Laura Ahearn, executive director of Parents for Megan's Law. "It's outrageous."

"We've got to make some purpose out of these kids who lose their lives to these perpetrators," said Erin Runion, mother of 5-year-old Samantha Runion, who was slain by a serial offender in July 2002.

Children's advocates claim that there are more than 550,000 registered sex offenders in the United States and that about one-fourth of them do not comply with the sex registry laws, and vanish when they get out of jail. What they don't say, however, is that the majority of these sex offenders are either relatives of the victims or close family friends, and that the percentage of stranger-against-stranger crimes is relatively low. However, it is usually only the stranger-against-stranger crimes that the public hears or reads about, which prompts many civil libertarians to voice their concern that the problem is overstated.

"What's often left out of this debate is that 90 percent of victims know their perpetrators," said Robert Perry, who is with the New York Civil Liberties Union. "These are family members, neighbors, acquaintances."

Nonetheless, during the height of the Duncan case,

Senator Charles Schumer, a Democrat from New York, began pushing for a national registry for sex offenders that would presumably close the loopholes that help repeat sex offenders to slip through the cracks.

In Idaho the push for tougher sex offender legislation is even more evident than nationally. In the latest Idaho legislative session, most new laws dealing with sex offenders were passed with little or no conversation—as long as there was not a price tag attached. Those laws that cost taxpayers money, however, didn't stand a chance, particularly since they were introduced in the 2006 election year. However, most new laws pertaining to sex offenders sailed right on through.

"With the current atmosphere, no one in their right mind is going to vote against anything that has to deal with sexual predators," said Senator Mike Jorgenson, a Republican from the Hayden Lake area who personally introduced several sex offender bills himself.

Another Republican politician, Senator John Goedde of Coeur d'Alene, is sponsoring the Buffer Zone Bill, which creates a five-hundred-foot shield or barrier around schools, in part because of the Duncan case, but also because of an incident involving a sex offender in Post Falls.

David "Coon" Merritt lived in Post Falls, and his home was known as a place where bored teenagers hung out. During the summer of 2000, Merritt took his 16-year-old son, Cody, and a neighbor, 14-year-old Carissa Benway, on a camping trip to Coeur d'Alene National Forest. While out in the woods, Merritt raped Carissa, and then murdered her with a butcher knife while his son watched. Cody later testified against his father, but Merritt worked out a deal in which he was sentenced to life in prison instead of the death penalty at a time when the state of Idaho did not want to spend the additional money it would take to seek a death sentence.

Carissa's mother, Bonnie Heilander, told her state representatives that she did not have any reason to suspect that Merritt, her neighbor, was a violent sex offender. She said that if she had known, she would not have allowed Carissa near him.

"If that [the Post Falls incident] had been the only issue, I would have had a tougher time getting that done [the Buffer Zone Bill]," Goedde said. "Obviously, the Groene case raised awareness."

A bill that passed unanimously will send sex offenders who have been designated as "violent sexual predators" to prison for life if they re-offend. The same bill had language written into it that called for increasing the minimum sentence from 5 to 15 years for repeat sex offenders who have not been so designated. Another bill that easily passed both the senate and the house in Idaho completely removed the statute of limitations for felony sexual abuse or lewd contact with a child.

"I think the work we did this session tightened up the violent sexual predator laws enough so it will be a deterrent," said Representative Jim Clark, a Republican from Hayden Lake. "It's a two strike, you're out system and it should be. The bar should be that high for sexual predators, or that low, depending on how you look at it."

Many states have a three-tier classification system for dealing with sex offenders, with violent sexual predators falling into the third tier for the most serious type. Idaho, however, only has a two-tier system, and a proposal for initiating a three-tier system failed before it could be introduced as a bill and voted upon by the legislature. Idaho currently has approximately 2,800 registered sex offenders, thirty-two of whom are designated as violent sexual predators who are likely to re-offend. The state could have benefited from a three-tier system, according to Thomas Hearn, chairman of the Idaho Sex Offender Classification Board.

"It would be a better use of our resources by separating the more dangerous from the less dangerous offenders," Hearn said recently when speaking in support of the three-tier system. "Why that idea didn't take off, I don't know."

"It appears that classification fell through the cracks," said Senator Goedde in describing how several articles of sex offender legislation were tossed around to see which bills would garner the most support from legislators. "There was a discussion, but to my knowledge a bill was never drafted. There were some issues involved, predominantly monetary."

Hearn explained that reclassifying 2,800 sex offenders would require expanding the Idaho Sex Offender Classification Board, at least for a period of time, because the board is now currently functioning due to the work of four volunteers and a secretary.

"We don't want the job of classifying a couple thousand sex offenders in the state unless you're going to put a staff in to go along with that," Hearn told reporters.

Representative Clark, who was a member of the original committee that set up the current sex offender classification system when the Community Right to Know Act was put in place in 1998, argued that there was nothing wrong with the current system and that it did not need to be overhauled.

"What we don't want to do is spend our time in court arguing and litigating on which tier they should be in," Clark said. "We keep it simple—we've got the worst, and the worst of the worst."

Goedde and Hearn did not agree with Clark's narrow-minded approach. Goedde argued that the system should be changed to three tiers by the next legislative session, and Hearn agreed.

"It will at least give us more awareness of who's more dangerous," Hearn said. "But that's something they have to decide. Are they going to spend the money? There was some progress made, but the problem is, most of the proposals that have money attached to them, they didn't want to do. . . . They did a lot of changes, but none that cost a lot of money. That's an ongoing struggle. How much financial investment do we want to make?"

The major flaw that Idaho lawmakers have been trying to correct is one in which the state has gone to great lengths to identify the worst, most violent sex offenders who are the most likely to re-offend, and then has allowed them to live virtually unsupervised in the community. The procedure requires them to come in to their local police station every three months and update their address information, and when they move, their photos are published in local newspapers. Otherwise they are free to go about their business unsupervised.

"We've seen some fairly bad people come across our desks," Hearn said. "These men are not being actively supervised. That, I think, is a huge gap and a significant problem as far as community protection."

According to Representative Marge Chadderdon, a Republican from Coeur d'Alene, a bill that didn't make it to the hearing stage was one that would have established lifetime electronic monitoring for certain offenders who were adjudged to be high-risk. The law would have been similar to Jessica's Law in Florida, but cost became an issue leading to its failure. Chadderdon was co-sponsor of Goedde's law requiring a five-hundred-foot buffer zone around schools, which, she said, wasn't an easy bill to get passed.

"It took four drafts before we even brought it to committee just to bring that little bill out," she said. "And then they amended it in the house and then amended it in the senate. I've grown to have a lot more respect for what we can do better with the funds we have right now."

Unlike Idaho's unsupervised "violent sexual predators," across the border in Washington, offenders who are classified as "sexually violent predators" are subject to indefinite civil commitment. Washington has kept 220 such offenders behind bars at its McNeil Island facility at a cost of more than $100,000 a year for each offender since its civil commitment law was passed in 1990. Idaho's legislature rejected such a law in 1998, in part because of its high cost. The issue of civil commitment also initially raised constitutional concerns, but the U.S. Supreme Court has upheld civil commitment laws in the states that have them.

In part because it was Washington that released Duncan back into the community, lawmakers in that state considered dozens of bills that would tighten the penalties and restrictions on sex offenders if passed. Sex-abuse victims filed in and out of hearings as they pleaded with lawmakers to do something to help stop the sexual abuse of children.

"The Duncan case was the heart of the thing," said Representative Al O'Brien, a retired Seattle police officer who ran many of the hearings. "When I heard that thing on the news, I was on the phone with my legal counsel and the criminal justice committee, talking about where we go from here."

"That case just stunned everybody," said Jim Hines, a salesman from Gig Harbor who is making a run for the Washington senate on a platform of tightening up sex offender laws. "It just makes citizens recoil," he said of the Duncan case.

It was particularly troubling to Hines that Duncan allegedly stalked his victims using night-vision goggles. It seemed like something right out of a horror movie.

"It literally sends chills up your spine," Hines said. Hines went on record saying that he would like to see all Level III sex offenders on electronic monitoring, as well as a year in prison for any offender who fails to register. He also wants to see a 25-year minimum sentence for sex offenders.

"Quit taking these tepid half-steps," Hines said. "Go with the measures that everybody knows the public wants."

O'Brien supported the 25-year minimum sentence.

"I wanted a long sentence in case we had another Duncan," O'Brien said.

"It affects the rest of the nation when people look at Duncan and the Groene case, and they want to do something about it," said Charles Onley, a representative for the Center for Sex Offender Management in Silver Spring, Maryland.

"Certainly, the state could go back and look at civil commitment if it chooses," said Idaho Deputy Attorney General Bill von Tagen. He also said that there were several other options that the state could consider, such as lifetime supervision for certain types of offenders, longer sentences and GPS-based electronic monitoring. "There are a lot of things that the state can do. A lot of them have a cost attached."

"We put collars on wolves, and we seem to be able to track them," said Senator Goedde. "I think that needs to be looked at. . . . The golf carts at the Circling Raven Golf Course have GPS on them, and if you get close to an environmentally sensitive area, an alarm goes off. So the technology is there to make someone conscious that they're not where they're supposed to be. And I can't believe that the same thing could not be done with a GPS monitoring system."

Troy King, attorney general from Alabama, recently had himself fitted with an electronic monitoring ankle bracelet and promised to wear it until the Alabama Legislature passes his bill that would require sex offenders to be on some type of GPS monitoring system for a minimum of 10 years following their release from prison.

"There's really nothing magic about GPS monitoring," said Roxanne Lieb, a researcher at the Washington State Institute for Public Policy. "You have to set the conditions, and then you have to have people who work for the state who monitor it and then go out and take action and investigate. It's more than just the cost of the instrument."

Even though many lawmakers cite cost as a factor in

their arguments against GPS monitoring, Pro Tech Monitoring, a Florida-based company that is a major vendor of GPS monitoring devices, claims that they can provide such a system for tracking offenders at a fraction of the cost of incarcerating them. Pro Tech claims that they can track an offender for approximately $10 a day, which works out to $3,650 annually, not including the cost of wages for state employees to monitor and follow up on the GPS reports. The cost in Idaho for housing a prisoner is approximately $18,000 a year.

What happens, however, when an offender cuts off the tracking device? It's a common question asked by lawmakers considering a move toward electronic tracking.

According to Steve Chapin, CEO of Pro Tech, authorities are notified immediately when an offender removes his tracking device. Chapin cited a case in which three offenders removed their monitors and tried to escape.

"Their probation officers were notified within one minute and took proper action," Chapin said. "They were all apprehended within forty-eight hours. . . . There's no such thing as something that is permanently affixed to somebody. So what we do is, we have very sophisticated tamper detection."

When Idaho initially enacted its sex offender registry law in 1993, the information was kept on file for law enforcement purposes only. Five years later, however, the legislature changed the law to allow full public access to the registry via the Internet, where anyone can search for an offender by name, zip code, or other criteria. The law was amended again in 2003 following the rape and murder of Carissa Benway, in part because she was the victim of a registered sex offender. The 2003 change to

the law stipulated that whenever a violent sexual predator relocated, their mug shots, descriptions of their
crimes and their new addresses would be published once
a week for three weeks in the newspapers in the locale of
their new residence. The sex offender must also pay for
a portion of the cost of publishing the information.

"A lot of times when people are looking at registries,
they think that the registry implies some form of supervision or accountability," said Charles Onley of the Center for Sex Offender Management. "But that doesn't
happen."

Idaho's registry, like the registries of most states,
doesn't make the promise that an offender is being supervised. Registries only state that public access "assists
the community in being observant of convicted sexual
offenders in order to prevent them from re-offending."
Idaho, as has been stated, only has two classifications to
its registry: one tier for violent sexual predators and a
lower tier for everyone else. The lower tier includes low-
risk statutory rape and incest offenders, people who
might benefit from treatment programs and offenders
who barely fall short of being "violent sexual predators." All registered offenders are required to re-register
once each year, but those deemed to be "violent sexual
predators" are required to re-register once every three
months.

"The limited resources we have available in Idaho need
to be focused on the higher-risk guys," said Hearn. "I
think that just makes sense, that we identify who those
people are and we pay attention to them. . . . In the
'everybody else' group, there are lots of people that are

dangerous guys ... but also in that mix there are some real low-risk guys and some real high-risk guys."

In a three-tier system, such as that used in Washington and other states, Level I offenders are considered the lowest possible risk to the community and are made up of people who have not shown predatory behavior; some in that category have also successfully completed treatment programs and have learned how to "stop" their sex offender behavior urges when they strike. Level II offenders are considered to be a moderate risk and are more likely to re-offend. Level III offenders pose the highest risk to the community and are most likely to re-offend if given the opportunity.

"Some sex offenders are very dangerous, very predatory, very likely to re-offend and need to be kept off the street or watched closely," Hearn said. "Other offenders are very low risk, and they don't need to be watched as closely. . . . I think the legislature has made good progress in lots of areas ... there was a lot of good legislation passed. There's more they could have done ... I want to go on record as saying that Idaho's new laws are good laws. But would they have prevented Duncan? No."

"Really, what this state needs to face is that it needs to quit spending money to incarcerate relatively nonviolent offenders and spend its resources on offenders that threaten society," said Robert Marsh, professor of criminal justice at Boise State University. "Registration was an idea that may be a good idea to inform the public, but it provides no guarantee that these crimes will not occur."

Hearn believes that there should be laws that prohibit a sex offender from being anywhere near where children congregate. However, other experts say that no law, no matter how stringent, can completely eliminate the risk to the public that sex offenders pose. Joseph Edward Duncan III is a good example. Duncan was released from prison in Washington where civil commitment laws are in place. His case was reviewed and he was considered a candidate for civil commitment, but in the end was not selected. When he left prison he moved to Fargo, North Dakota, jumped bail on a new charge in neighboring Minnesota and went to Idaho, where he allegedly wreaked havoc and literally destroyed a family. A law prohibiting sex offenders from being near children simply would not have worked in Duncan's case—he proved that he would re-offend when given the opportunity.

"No matter what system we put in place," von Tagen said, "police, prosecutors, parents, everyone that's concerned with the welfare of kids or law enforcement needs to use it. Because if the system isn't being used properly, if people aren't convicted of the right offenses, if people are let out of jail on insufficient bail or something like that, the system's going to break down."

In May 2006, the U.S. Senate passed a bill that would strengthen sex offender registry requirements at the national level. The bill, S. 1086, makes sex offender registration mandatory in all states as long as its provisions do not violate a state's constitution. It was passed in part because of the Duncan case.

"More stringent national registration requirements for sex offenders, especially violent sex offenders, will reduce the likelihood that the terrible events of last summer in north Idaho could ever be repeated," said Idaho Senator Mike Crapo, Republican co-sponsor of the bill.

"Sharing this information across state lines provides a strong network that can be cross-referenced by law enforcement and parents as communities nationwide work together to ensure the safety of all children."

S. 1086 is expected to be considered by the U.S. House of Representatives in the near future.

Another Idaho bill, SB 1414, expanded the amount of money the state would spend for the treatment of victims' mental health from $2,500 to $25,000. The idea for that bill came about when lawmakers learned that Shasta Groene only stood to receive $2,500 for her treatment, and when they considered all that she had been through and would likely go through in the months and years that would follow.

"What gave me the most satisfaction with that bill is, everybody wanted to come up with stiffer sentencing and punishment," said Senator Jorgenson. "But this was the one bill that dealt with the victims and trying to help them out."

—CHAPTER TWENTY-EIGHT—

I F IT WERE POSSIBLE THAT ANYTHING GOOD OR POSITIVE could come out of a case as tragic as this one, it is that it helped raise the public's awareness about monsters like Joseph Edward Duncan III, and inspired adults to discuss abuse and crimes of pedophilia and murder with children. Although the case is reprehensible, depressing and beyond the comprehension of most people, it nonetheless provided an opportunity for parents and children's and victims' rights advocates to open up and teach kids what is normal behavior by an adult and what is not.

"When tragedies such as this happen, it's a wonderful time to open up dialogue," said Tinka Schaffer, development director for Children's Village in Coeur d'Alene. " 'Mommy and Daddy are here to protect you. We never want anyone to hurt you.' Role model, pretend," Schaffer advises.

"They announced a missing child at Wal-Mart the other day and I picked up my daughter immediately and wouldn't let her go," said one area parent. "She's pretty, and if they want a kid bad enough, they'll get them."

The parent said that she would like to take Schaffer up on her advice, but her daughter is only 17 months old. She indicated that she would definitely teach her daughter the kinds of things that Schaffer recommends when she gets a little older, but for now the best thing to do is protect her daughter, in part by not letting her out of her sight.

"There's a fine line between teaching a child to grow up on her own and making her careless or neurotic," said the parent.

Much of what was being talked about in the aftermath of the northern Idaho tragedy focused on "good touch" and "bad touch," and "body respect" in general. A parent from Spokane told reporters that the recent news about Duncan and the Groene case has prompted her to watch her $2^{1}/_{2}$-year-old son much more closely and to pay particular attention to anyone who has any interaction with him.

Nancy Taylor, a city councilwoman and parent from Hayden, Idaho, became a sex abuse education advocate following the molestation of one of her own children several years earlier. She was responsible for getting a link to the state's sex offender registry added to the City of Hayden website, and is hopeful that the Duncan case will prompt people to be more proactive in their approach to understanding and dealing with child sexual abuse.

"It's really hard to protect your kids," Taylor said. "Teach them to yell, scream. Being proactive of where they go is not enough. You have to know the people they're with. The Groene case is raising awareness and that's good. These are our kids being damaged for life, and it's perpetuating. How many molesters were molested as children?"

Between July 1, 2004, and June 30, 2005, the Kootenai

County prosecutor's office brought twenty-eight criminal charges related to child sexual abuse. According to Prosecutor Bill Douglas, those twenty-eight cases were only a small percentage of the number of actual sexual abuse complaints that were filed, because his office is only able to prosecute the cases that have the greatest potential for obtaining a conviction.

"The dynamics [of child sexual abuse cases] are perhaps similar to domestic violence, the silent crime," Douglas said. "These are crimes where the offender manipulates the victim into not reporting. There are threats, delayed reporting," among the reasons why they are designated "silent" crimes. However, Douglas is quick to point out that such cases in Kootenai County have doubled in the past ten years.

"We are trending up and I think it's because victims of crime are making more reports, because of greater confidence in the criminal justice system that this crime will be addressed and that justice will be served," Douglas said.

Another problem that victims, their families, counselors and the criminal justice system face is that children who are victimized often are saddled with guilt feelings that they somehow caused the abuse to occur, according to Sandra Turtle, a counselor in Coeur d'Alene who has been involved in helping children deal with the terrible ordeal of sexual abuse for more than a decade.

"You have to help them see that they didn't [cause the abuse]," said Turtle. "They have to at least get angry that something was taken from them, and then there's recovery."

If children don't get the help they need to get them

through the recovery process, depression and anxiety often set in and the victims, sometimes later in life, will seek ways to help them feel better even if those ways are only temporary, unreal and not beneficial or conducive to recovery. Sometimes victims venture into the use of drugs, alcohol, gambling and impulsive buying, thinking that these things will help them feel better about themselves. Some also develop eating disorders, and others become self-destructive and attempt suicide.

"If a child has someone to tell when they're young and they know that they'll be believed, it can almost be resolved then," Turtle said.

One of the things that parents can do to help detect whether sexual abuse has occurred or is currently ongoing within a family, according to Turtle, is to observe how their children react around others. If the child becomes ill at ease, perturbed or reserved when in the presence of a particular relative, friend or neighbor, the child should probably be questioned about why they are reacting in such a manner. A book on the subject of child sexual abuse that is recommended by Turtle and other counselors is *Good-Touch/Bad-Touch*, by Pam Church.

Tinka Schaffer has been recommending that school districts place sex abuse prevention in their curricula, and some schools are already doing so.

"It doesn't have to be negative," Schaffer said. "Just preventative. They can talk about it like nutrition and dental care. It's not rocket scientist stuff."

It is important and encouraging to note that since the Groene tragedy, coupled with the ability of people like Duncan to slip through the cracks of the system, technological corporations are beginning to help with regard to the dissemination of information about missing children. One such company, SurferQuest, which supplies approximately 1,000 computer kiosks at various locations throughout the U.S., has begun donating its screen space so that the National Center for Missing and Exploited Children can get their information about missing children into public view in yet another format or venue. SurferQuest's kiosks provide public Internet access for a fee and can be found at hotels, cafes, or other public locations. When a kiosk is not being used by a customer, photographs of missing children and their descriptions appear on the screens in space that is normally used for advertising. There's also no cost to the customer when information about a missing child is requested, or reported, through their sites.

"It's really important to give a missing child as much exposure as we can after the abduction," said Kathryn Koning, SurferQuest's president and a mother of four. Koning estimated that more than 300,000 people can view SurferQuest's images of missing children each day.

"We know that pictures work," said D'Ann Taflin, spokeswoman for the National Center for Missing and Exploited Children. According to Taflin, one in six missing children whose photos are advertised is eventually found.

—CHAPTER TWENTY-NINE—

ONE YEAR AFTER THE TRAGEDY OF A CASE THAT ROCKED the Pacific Northwest and grabbed the attention of the entire nation, the surviving members of the Groene and McKenzie families still struggled to make some sense out of what had happened to their loved ones as they tried in vain to put their own lives back together. A year after their brutal murders, Mark McKenzie and Brenda Groene were remembered by friends and family as a hard-working couple who liked to party and who had planned to get married someday. In the year since the tragedy struck, both families, according to Brenda's mother, Darlene Torres, had worked consistently to try to restore Brenda's and Mark's reputations, which had been tarnished after law enforcement personnel had revealed that they both had methamphetamine and marijuana in their blood at the time of their deaths.

"The most frustrating part was to have to fight for their honor when it shouldn't have been that way in the first place," Torres told a reporter at the *Spokesman-Review*.

Torres recalled the day in March 2006 that the family celebrated what would have been Slade's 14th birthday, when everyone, including Shasta, showed up at the house on Frontage Road and released balloons into the air in his honor. She said that it was probably difficult for most people to understand how family members could ever go back to the house where their loved ones had been brutally murdered.

"That's where their home was," Torres said. "That's where all of us would have been for his birthday."

"Slade was just getting to the age where you could do real fun things with him," said Steve McKenzie. "You could take him hunting. You could take him hiking. And he could keep up."

Ralph McKenzie tearfully recalled fond memories of his son when they had gone on hunting trips. Even though Mark is gone, Ralph still expects to see him come running into one of their favorite hunting camps in the mountains around Coeur d'Alene, asking everyone if they had seen any deer or elk, and looking for a cold beer in one of the ice chests. But he knows that it will never happen. Except for his memory of happier times, those days are gone forever, stolen, according to the police, by Joseph Edward Duncan III.

Although the pain of the tragedy has not gone away, Lee McKenzie Wood, Mark's mother, finds some solace when she is able to talk about her son and his family.

"I feel better when I can talk about it 'cause Mark is there," Lee said. "Brenda's there. They're both there, and the kids."

Lee felt very close to Brenda Groene, and praised her as a good mother and a great cook who did her best to take care of her family. She said that she considered Brenda's children as her own grandchildren.

"Mark loved those kids," Lee said. "Every one of those kids, as far as he was concerned, they were his own."

Lee described her son as being physically fit, able to carry his own in just about any situation that demanded physical strength and stamina. She wondered why he had not been able to overpower someone like Duncan.

"Mark would pack a quarter of an elk out of the mountains without any problem," she said. "I can't figure out how Duncan got the advantage over Mark and Brenda."

Regarding the recent news reports that Steve Groene, in part due to his recurrence of throat cancer, was considering changing his initial demands that Duncan receive a death penalty trial, instead asking the prosecutor to plea bargain, Lee said that she would have to disagree with his choice. Even though she said that she loves Shasta like her own granddaughter and understands the trauma that putting the child on the witness stand would entail, she nonetheless wants Duncan to receive the death penalty.

"He never gave the McKenzie family a choice, so why should we give him a choice?" Lee asked. "He's got death coming to him one way or another, and if he gets life, I hope that someone in prison does him in."

Ralph McKenzie remains the legal owner of the property on Frontage Road where the murders occurred, and it is his desire to have the house torn down and the land it sits on turned into a wetland. However, because the prosecution will likely want to take the jury on a tour of the house, he will probably have to wait until after Duncan's trial to complete his plans.

Steve Groene, meanwhile, has been organizing biker rallies when not making appearances on Oprah Winfrey's and Geraldo Rivera's shows to push his agenda for tougher laws against sex offenders like Duncan. An outspoken advocate for Dylan's Law, Groene has worked relentlessly while battling his own health problems to get the tougher laws passed.

"Hopefully, Washington will get it [Dylan's Law] passed and maybe set the precedent on that," Groene said.

"I'd like to see this guy get his just desert," Groene continued, "but if we could find out about some other crimes or other things by doing a plea bargain with this guy, I think that's a better route to go."

On the dark anniversary of the tragedy that turned his life upside down, Steve Groene asked the public that had reached out so willingly, even eagerly, to help him and Shasta for an additional favor.

"Just say a prayer," he asked, "and wish that everybody would say a prayer for 'em . . . we know they're sitting with God right now, and we think he's taking good care of 'em. They deserve it."

BOB HOLLINGSWORTH, THE WOLF LODGE NEIGHBOR WHO first reported that something was terribly wrong at the McKenzie residence, looks at the grass that Slade Groene had mowed along his driveway a year earlier, a job for which he never got paid, despite Hollingsworth's attempts to deliver the money. The ordeal forever changed his life, as well as that of his wife.

"I went to the door and saw that door and that porch," Hollingsworth recently recalled to a *Spokesman-Review* reporter. "I butcher lambs and I know what real blood looks like. I knew somebody had been murdered here."

Hollingsworth, who refers to himself as "an accidental, integral part of this case," said that he wouldn't mind if the house where the murders occurred was torn down.

"It affects you," he said. "My wife, it affects her a lot. She doesn't say much, but I think it affects her a lot. She wishes that house was gone over there."

"You wouldn't be human if it didn't impact you in some way," said Captain Ben Wolfinger. "Everybody who had a part in it was impacted in some way, shape or form."

"It has affected people's feelings of security in their homes," agreed Prosecutor Bill Douglas. "People take more precautions now to lock their doors. The randomness, I think, invaded a lot of people's sense of security and brought out a lot of change."

"It has changed the way I look at strangers," said a Spokane resident. "I wonder who I am sitting next to at the theater, who is in the grocery line ahead of me. Could it be some deranged killer?"

"That's especially true in a rural or frontier community where everybody knows everybody, or at least knows their best friend," said Ann Kirkwood, a research associate at the Idaho/Wyoming Center for Rural, Frontier and Tribal Health, which is part of the National Child Traumatic Stress Network. "Here, you have the illusion that it's safe."

Some parents have taken precautions in the form of giving their children cellular telephones to use, so that they can call home when they arrive at school and when they leave to come home in the afternoon.

"I've always been concerned, but it got more intense after what happened in north Idaho last year," said one parent who gave his child a cell phone to use. "It's like part of life now. It's just like if she was going to have cereal every morning for breakfast. She knows that she has to call dad."

Recently, a friend of the victims' families began selling bumper stickers and other merchandise that contains a very strong anti–sex-offender message. The one that seems to have received the most attention is a bumper sticker that reads, "KILL DUNCAN!" They have been showing up on cars in 2006, and someone placed one on the "ABSOLUTELY NO TRESPASSING" sign that has been posted at the Groene–McKenzie home since the murders.

Despite all of the anti-Duncan sentiment being expressed across northern Idaho, the citizens of the area have done a remarkable job of pulling together through hope and compassion for each other.

"One of the things we learned was that we needed to take care of ourselves and each other," said Lana Hamilton, principal of Fernan Elementary School, which Shasta and Dylan attended. "We experienced a unique bond as a result of the events. The entire Fernan community was affected—students, staff and families."

One person, a grandmother from Spokane who had been visiting Coeur d'Alene the day before Shasta was rescued, recalled that she believes that she had encountered Duncan and Shasta at a Subway sandwich shop. Although she hadn't reported the encounter at the time, she said that she had learned something from the ordeal.

"I went in there [Subway] and there was this dirtball of a guy in line," said the grandmother. "He was just a mess. And then I went into the restroom and there was this little girl standing there and she was just washing her hands . . . I looked right into this girl's eyes. It was like she was trying to tell me something."

The woman said that she was embarrassed that she didn't tell someone of her encounter, of which she is "99.9 percent sure it was them." She even saw a red Jeep in the Subway shop's parking lot, just like the one Duncan had been driving when apprehended at the Denny's restaurant. The woman said that it wasn't until after Shasta had been rescued and Duncan's photos had appeared in the newspapers two days later that she was certain it was them she had seen.

"If anything like that ever happens again," said the grandmother, "I'll say, 'What's your name?' I had my cell phone. I could have called. I could have kept her in the bathroom . . . I could have saved her from another day in hell."

—CHAPTER THIRTY—

It was recently revealed that a planned memorial for Dylan Groene consisting of three stones that will depict his name, birth date and the date he died will be placed at the Montana campsite in the Lolo National Forest where he was killed, to replace a makeshift memorial that Shasta and Steve Groene left at the site during the summer of 2005. Shasta had previously scrawled Dylan's name on a rock with "1995–2005," with an arrow pointing to the dates. She had also written, "YEARS HE LIVED." Shasta and her father had also placed Dylan's shoes, along with some toys, near the rock, and a poem titled "I'm an Angel Now Daddy" that was written by Steve Groene. The poem will also be engraved onto the new memorial, and native perennials will be planted around it.

The small Montana community of St. Regis is still reeling in the aftermath of Duncan's reign of terror. Following his arrest, many St. Regis residents recognized the photographs of Duncan and the children in the newspapers and realized that they had seen him. Some residents recognized the children, and realized that Duncan had brought them into town on a few occasions, sometimes eating at a local hamburger restaurant. Many residents felt a lot of guilt because they had not recognized Duncan and the children sooner.

Shortly after Shasta was rescued, the Western Montana Mental Health Center and the Mineral County Public Health began holding counseling sessions for members of the community who felt they needed help. "After they saw the children's pictures in the news and after that little boy was killed, people recognized them and they felt a lot of guilt," said Peggy Stevens, a public health nurse.

"So many people have just been beating themselves up about not noticing they were up there," said John Q. Murray, editor of a weekly newspaper, the *Clark Fork Chronicle*, which is distributed in western Montana. Murray is responsible for overseeing the fundraising efforts for Dylan's memorial and its placement at the site.

"I was telling everyone about how emotional it was when I visited up there," Murray said. "It was like getting punched in the gut. I wanted to sink to my knees."

Murray now publishes the local sex offender registry as well as Amber Alerts in the *Clark Fork Chronicle*.

IN THE SPRING OF 2006, STEVE GROENE BEGAN INDICATING that he did not want Shasta to have to face Duncan in court and testify against him, despite the fact that he had previously said that Duncan deserves death.

"This guy took four lives, and unfortunately we can only kill him once," Groene said in an interview with Oprah Winfrey in the autumn of 2005. "Family members ought to be allowed to inflict death on somebody sentenced to death."

Duncan has also publicly announced that he doesn't

want Shasta to have to take the witness stand against him. According to his attorney, Public Defender John Adams, Duncan and Adams's office are "one hundred percent behind Steve Groene and his attempts to reach a settlement in the case to protect his family. We share those concerns and Mr. Duncan shares those concerns. . . . Mr. Duncan doesn't want Shasta to spend the next ten to twenty years in courtrooms, watching the trial and appellate trial and being twenty years old and having to come back to court again."

Upon hearing of Duncan's concerns, Steve McKenzie told reporters that he doesn't care what Duncan says or thinks.

"I would think his concern is B.S.," McKenzie said. "If he has any concern, it's for himself. I would doubt he would care about her safety."

"Nobody wants her to testify," Prosecutor Bill Douglas said. "But my responsibility calls me to call her. My interest is in representing the community."

Although Douglas had not seen videotapes of recent interviews Shasta had with Geraldo Rivera, in which Rivera had described Shasta as "one of America's bravest" victims, Douglas, while making it clear that he was not criticizing Steve Groene, told reporters that Shasta's father's actions seemed contradictory to him.

"The two could come into conflict," Douglas said, "but I hope they do not. I think as her parent, he's in the best position to make decisions for her."

Douglas indicated that Shasta's willingness and ability to talk to a national audience on television was a good indicator that she could be a good witness in court.

"The fact that she's able to relate to a large audience

bodes well for her ability to testify in a courtroom," Douglas said. "I want the chance to sit down with other family members to make sure they know this case is on track and to invite any comments and reactions they may have to Steve's feelings. That doesn't mean we're not going to have a trial. . . . That's all I can say."

THE WHITE CINDERBLOCK HOUSE ON FRONTAGE ROAD WAS once the childhood home of Ralph McKenzie, Mark's father. He lived there for more than twenty-five years and went to school nearby. Now it's difficult for him to return to the home that has remained in the family for decades, and it is his wish that the property become a wetland preserve, an idea that formed from a conversation with officials at the U.S. Army Corps of Engineers. Someone with the Corps had mentioned that the property was a "great wetland," and McKenzie liked the idea.

"I said, 'If you think so, build it,'" McKenzie said recently. He said that Wolf Lodge Creek had a somewhat regular history of overflowing its banks, and that he had tried for years to keep its floodwaters in check. In addition to the U.S. Army Corps of Engineers, the Idaho Fish and Game department is assessing the feasibility of whether Frontage Road property could be made part of a larger project to help protect the area's native fish.

"It's an important migration corridor and rearing area for cutthroat trout," said Kathy Cousins, an Idaho Fish and Game department biologist. "We're very interested in trying to preserve that."

According to McKenzie, the department said that it normally wouldn't try to acquire such a small parcel.

However, there are possibilities if the site was part of something larger and included conservation easements or habitat improvement programs along the banks of Wolf Lodge Creek and, beyond the property, Cedar Creek.

"My intention is to go and meet with the other landowners in the area to get the feel of what they're comfortable with," Cousins said. "This 5.5-acre parcel could act as a very good public access point if it were a part of a larger project. . . . Right now it's really in its infancy. We're just investigating the potential."

Cousins said that a memorial at the site might also be considered if the idea moves forward into the planning stages.

Because of the flooding and wetlands characteristics of the property, "It's not a good place for a house, regardless of what happened there, which is, of course, an awful thing," said Idaho Department of Lands Director Winston Wiggins.

As word that the property might be for sale got around, the Idaho Transportation Department also expressed interest. A federal "wetland banking" program has a provision that allows state transportation departments to restore wetlands near a highway project that has disturbed adjacent wetlands.

"If it was offered, the department would be interested in investigating it further," said Idaho Transportation Department spokesperson Jeff Stratten. "We've purchased small parcels in the past, and then enhanced or developed the wetlands to meet environmental requirements."

"The crime left the home in bad condition," said Detective Brad Maskell, despite the efforts of a professional biohazard cleanup crew that removed flooring, walls and virtually "anything that was contaminated [with blood and bodily fluids] during the crime."

According to Steve McKenzie, the family had originally planned to keep the property. They cleaned up the outside area by mowing the yard and getting rid of the tall weeds, but ultimately changed their minds because of what had occurred there.

"I was not happy being there," he said. "I was very uncomfortable. It was always like home. It was always where you went, and it doesn't feel like that anymore."

Ralph McKenzie said that he would only consider selling the property if the purchasers were willing to go along with his wetlands preserve idea.

THE AVERAGE PERSON WHO HAS NEVER BEEN FACED WITH the devastating effects of a local child murder really has no idea how such a tragedy affects a community as a whole. But residents of Beaumont, California, made it very clear just how much a child murder can transform an entire town when several residents traveled from Riverside County to Coeur d'Alene in the autumn of 2005 to recognize Amber Deahn, the Denny's waitress who'd played a role in Shasta's rescue and Duncan's apprehension. For nearly ten years a Beaumont woman had kept a yellow ribbon attached to her refrigerator as a remembrance of Anthony Martinez's abduction and murder with the hope in the back of her mind that the boys killer would someday be identified and apprehended. She presented the yellow ribbon, its color now faded, to Amber, who proudly pinned it to her shirt.

"It means a lot that in Beaumont we no longer have to

look at our neighbor and say, 'Is that the guy who did it?' " said David Castaldo, a former president of the Beaumont/Cherry Valley Rotary Club.

The group of southern California representatives also brought Deahn proclamations from the California legislature hailing her as a hero, and presented her with an 8-foot-long banner depicting a photograph of a smiling Anthony Martinez. It was signed with messages of gratitude by hundreds of citizens from the Beaumont community.

"Thanks for the big help," read one message. "This means so much to me. You caught the guy that took my best friend away. So thank you so much."

"You have helped bring many answers to my family," wrote Diana Medina, Anthony's mother. Medina was the first person to sign the banner.

Lieutenant Mitch White, one of the primary investigators in the case, couldn't bring himself to retire until Anthony's murder was solved. White was also in the party that traveled to Coeur d'Alene.

"You brought closure to a lot of people, including me," White said to Deahn. "I've been looking for Anthony's killer since 1997. It's finally to an end."

Charla Sparks, Anthony's third-grade teacher, presented Deahn with a baby book, *Pat the Bunny*, for Deahn's 6-week-old baby boy.

"Anthony was my boy," Sparks told Deahn. She said that she volunteered to answer calls on a tip line from 2 to 4 A.M. after Anthony was abducted. "People never dreamed our little town would suffer anything like this. It's beyond understanding."

"I was glad to be given the opportunity to do what I did," Deahn said. "My heart goes out to his mother. I'm glad, if for nothing else, she's able to have some closure and peace."

—CHAPTER THIRTY-ONE—

ACCORDING TO REPORTS BY THE ASSOCIATED PRESS AND
the *Coeur d'Alene Press*, two letters purportedly
written by Joseph Edward Duncan III were placed on Internet auction sites that specialize in selling items related to serial killers in late 2005. Bidding for one of the
letters on www.murderauction.com started at $20. It
was believed that the two letters were sold shortly after
appearing on the Internet.

Victims' advocate Andy Kahan, who works in the
Houston, Texas, mayor's office, said that Duncan's notoriety had placed him in the same classification as serial
killers such as Angel Ramirez, Dennis Rader, Albert
DeSalvo, Charles Manson and John Wayne Gacy. Kahan's concern is that Duncan himself might be profiting
from the sales of his own "murderabilia."

"We're of the bizarre opinion that criminals should
not be able to rape, rob and murder and then turn around
and make a buck out of it," Kahan said.

Kahan said that he believed that both letters, which
had turned up in a period of less than a month, had sold.
Both were handwritten.

"They usually re-post them if they haven't sold," he

said. Kahan believed the first letter sold for $50. "My best guess is that the letters will be a hot commodity."

A part of the first letter showed the upper left-hand of the return address on the envelope and appeared to have an authentic return address from the Kootenai County jail. The end portion of the letter was posted and it read, in part:

> . . . wanted to post your own comments to the blog [illegible] were antagonistic as long as they were honest & we'd have to talk about that of course if this plays out at all. So let me know what you think. Please write back as soon as you can & remember no stamps, they only allow paper and simple (no glue) cards and photos (no Polaroids). So its best to keep it simple and just send letters. Thanks again for writing and for your support.

The letter was signed "Jet," the nickname Duncan developed for himself using the initials from Joseph Edward the Third. The letter continued.

> P.S. Please call me "Jet" But address letters to Joseph Duncan.
> P.P.S. Can you type fast? I have a lot to blog about!

The last sentence was followed by a smiley face.

Kahan, who has worked with crime victims from all parts of the country since 1992, tries, often in vain, to keep criminals from profiting from their crimes and notoriety. He said that there are sales of killer memorabilia all over the Internet.

"And somebody's making a buck off of it," he said.

He said that a recent pencil sketch of a dog purportedly drawn by Dennis Rader, the so-called BTK (Bind, Torture, Kill) Killer was placed on the Internet and opened at auction for $1. Fifty-four bids later it was sold for $179.10. Kahan would like to see legislation nationally that would allow states to seize the profits from "murderabilia," even from third-party dealers. He believes the money should be given to the victims' families.

"The killers are glorified and this continues to keep them in the public eye," he said. "That's just not right."

MEANWHILE, IN PART BECAUSE OF THE DUNCAN CASE, California Governor Arnold Schwarzenegger has jumped on the sex offender legislation bandwagon and has proposed a requirement that paroled sex offenders be required to wear satellite tracking devices for life, according to the Associated Press. He also wants to prohibit registered sex offenders from living near parks and schools, and is proposing legislation that would increase penalties for possession of child pornography, date rape and using the Internet to lure minors for sex acts.

"I'm sponsoring this legislation to give California the strictest laws and toughest penalties for the worst crimes," Schwarzenegger said at a news conference within a month of Duncan's apprehension. "We want to give greater protection for all Californians—especially our children—against sexual offenders."

Schwarzenegger's proposals, while well-meaning, could be cost-prohibitive. Democrats in the state senate rejected a bill in June 2005 that would have required lifetime electronic tracking of convicted pedophiles.

"I don't know how we digest a fifty-two-page bill and give it the appropriate attention when we have as many things going on as we do," said Assemblyman Mark Leno, a Democrat from San Francisco who is chairperson of the state's public safety committee.

Leno said that placing all registered sex offenders under satellite surveillance for life would be very expensive, and estimated that Schwarzenegger's package of proposed changes, formally titled the Sexual Predator Punishment and Control Act, could cost as much as $500 million a year for the satellite surveillance, additional jail time for offenders who violated conditions of their parole, and longer parole terms.

Leno also argued that placing limits on where a registered sex offender can live could create problems. He cited a person that he knew of who had committed a sex offense more than thirty years ago but had never again gotten into trouble. He questioned whether it would be fair to people like that who stood to lose their apartment or home under the proposed changes because they lived near a park or a school.

"Is this good public policy?" Leno asked. "I think not."

IN THE AFTERMATH OF THE DUNCAN CASE, OFFICIALS WITH the city of Melbourne, Florida, announced that they would begin keeping tabs on that city's sexual predators twice as often as required by Florida law. In November 2005, the Melbourne City Council decided to force sex offenders living in that city to register their home addresses, employment status, vehicle registration and other personal information with police officials every three months instead of every six months. The tougher stance against sex offenders is designed to work hand-in-hand with a future police officer who will be assigned to a full-time sexual violator beat.

"It's not easy putting residency restrictions on anybody," said Councilman Mark LaRusso. "We're not moving anyone from their homes. We're not going out and taking anybody to the woodshed."

Under the new rules, which were approved unanimously, sex offenders will have to register in person with city police and the Brevard County Sheriff's Office, depending upon where they reside.

Melbourne officials scratched earlier plans that would have doubled the state-mandated residency restrictions for some predators and offenders, which would have forced them to live 2,000 feet from schools, daycare centers and public parks instead of 1,000 feet, the required distance already in place. The concerns that prompted them to scrap their plans were potential enforcement difficulties and future lawsuits.

Denise Hughes-Conlon, president of the Florida Association for the Treatment of Sexual Abusers, said that she had opposed the 2,000-foot idea.

"As a professional working with this population," she said, "my hope is the population of the community become educated and realize the biggest danger to their children aren't the people on the Internet registries. They're the people who haven't been arrested yet."

—EPILOGUE—

JOSEPH EDWARD DUNCAN III HAS BEEN HELD WITHOUT BAIL awaiting trial since his arrest at the Denny's in Coeur d'Alene the night Shasta was rescued. In January 2006 he received a letter from a Vancouver, Washington, woman named Jean, a staunch supporter of Initiative 921, which calls for a "one strike" law that would lock up violent sex offenders for life. In her letter to Duncan, she condemned him for being a child molester. Duncan responded to Jean the following month. His letter, which was made public, began:

> Dear Jean,
> "Without forgiveness there is only insanity."
> I hope that you are not too dismayed to receive letters from me. Normally I would not reply to such a rage filled letters, [sic] but I honestly saw genuine pain behind your words and I felt you at least deserved some kind of answer.

Duncan wrote that God had been speaking with him "everyday" [sic] since his arrest, and denied being "crazy." He insisted that he was not "hearing voices," and portrayed his capture at the Denny's restaurant as surrendering to the authorities according to instructions from God. He wrote that it was God speaking to him and not Satan "because not even the devil himself" would have been able to cause him to turn himself in to his "most feared and hated enemy (the system)." He also claimed that it was God who had "asked" him to write to Jean to inform her that God's forgiveness is "for everyone. . . . God's power is his forgiveness, if he can't forgive me then he is weak and not God at all! Is that what you really believe?"

In the letter, Duncan repeatedly told Jean that he understood that she was "hurt and angry." But he claimed that her letter had hurt *him*, and that his "own anger, pain and confusion" about "what happened" was greater "than anyone's," with the possible exception of the victims' families. The most important thing, he declared, was to prevent future losses of innocent life:

> Right now how other people feel is much more important to me than my own feelings. But, as a society, we need to focus on the future "Dylans," the ones who also deserve nothing but the best in life, before they too loose (sic) it to some hate filled person who wants to "play god" by judging those around him instead of taking responsibility for their own feelings! The question should not be "WHY, WHY?" but rather "how can I help stop this from happening again?"

He claimed that he would be willing to sacrifice his own life if it would help: "If dying, even going to hell, would erase all that had happened, then I would volunteer in a moment. But it can't . . ."

The letter concluded with a plea to society to reach out with forgiveness to angry men like himself:

> Our fear and hatred is the sickness and there is no "good hatred." If you continue to hate me, and even kill me, then you send a message to other "sex offenders" in this country. I HATE YOU! And I wish you were DEAD! You need to honestly ask yourself how that message will affect them the next time they see a vulnerable person who represents to them exactly what I represent to you!
>
> . . . .I hope and pray to God that this letter helps, even if in the smallest way, to alleviate your pain. It is so important to me that people understand Gods presence and power in all that happens. . . . Just open your heart to God. A good way to start is to open your heart to someone you hate (not necessarily me). These are the kind of things God has been telling me about. I hope they help you understand, so you can help us all heal, and stop the insanity!

Many of those who read the letter, both before it was made public and afterward, doubt that Duncan deliberately allowed himself to be caught that night at Denny's.

"I think what he's doing there is just manipulating the circumstances after the fact in order to cast himself in a better light," said Mike Schuler, one of the organizers of Initiative 921, a Washington state initiative to make it easier for authorities to keep sexual predators behind bars for life. "I don't think he was on his way to turn himself in or bring Shasta home or anything. I think he got caught. . . . There's a certain percentage of these guys who commit violent sex offenses that are just not curable. There's no point in trying to rehabilitate them, it's just a waste of time trying to rehabilitate them . . . [to] turn them loose back in society where they're going to commit another crime."

In the aftermath of the tragedies surrounding this sad story, Steve Groene, still battling recurring throat cancer that reappeared following surgery, was admitted to a Seattle hospital in early October 2005, less than two weeks before jury selection for Duncan's trial was to begin. His vocal chords and a cancerous tumor were removed, according to a spokesperson at the University of Washington Medical Center. According to Groene's sister, Wendy Price, his prognosis is good. He had plans to return to Idaho for his recovery.

Before his latest surgery, Groene was often at the forefront of organized campaign efforts that support stiffer sentences for sex offenders.

"This is the only thing out there that has some teeth," Groene told the press. It has been dubbed "Dylan's Law," much like the initiative in New Jersey years earlier that was called "Megan's Law." Yard sales were being held around the state at the time of writing to raise money to hire people to gather the required 225,000 signatures to get the initiative on the ballot in November 2006.

The initiative, if passed by voters, would mandate life in prison without parole for a number of sex crimes, including child rape and first-degree child molestation.

"The deadline is looming and we need many people on board now," said Tracy Oetting, author of the initiative, who has attempted twice before to get a one-strike sex offender initiative passed.

"There's just this overflow of sexual terrorism in our

country, and nobody's doing anything about it," said one of the initiative's organizers.

Steve Groene, on the other hand, thinks there's a better way to deal with sex offenders because, he said, life in prison seems too soft for them.

"I think these guys should be taken out and shot on sight," Groene said. "There's no doubt that they're going to re-offend."

According to Groene, Shasta, now 9, is doing well and does not talk much about what happened to her and Dylan during their weeks of captivity with Duncan. At her own request, Shasta returned to the same school that she and Dylan had attended prior to their abduction, and is getting good grades in her classes. She plays soccer, swims regularly and has taken up horseback riding.

Meanwhile, lawmakers in the state of Washington have passed several bills during the winter months of 2005 and 2006 that take aim at sex offenders, mostly because of Duncan's actions. Among the provisions passed into law are requirements for electronic monitoring of some sex offenders following their release from prison, increasing minimum sentences for some sex crimes to 25 years, and tougher penalties for failing to abide by the sex offender registration requirements. Lawmakers also passed a new category of offense, "criminal trespass against children," to allow law enforcement to ban sex offenders from parks, swimming pools, playgrounds and any other such sites that children are known to frequent.

A number of prosecutors, as well as those involved in victims' advocacy groups, largely disagree with the passage of one-strike types of laws, saying that it would be a mistake to have a "one-size-fits-all" prison sentence for sex crimes. Their argument is that if the punishment is too severe, people will shy away from reporting friends or relatives who commit sex crimes.

"For the stranger rapist and the serial child molester, I don't think there's any disagreement about what we need to do with those people," said Tom McBride, executive secretary of the Washington Association of Prosecuting Attorneys. "But that's not the majority of cases."

According to McBride, most serious sex crimes are already "two strikes" crimes, where the laws in place have been effective in putting the offender in prison for life for the second offense. With Washington already having sex offender laws that are among the toughest in the nation, people like McBride question the need for a "one-strike" law, which Dylan's Law would effectively accomplish. Opponents believe that such a law might only serve to put the offender deeper into the closet or into hiding, committing more offenses that go unreported in the process, instead of getting the help that those offenders who are amenable to treatment would receive.

In May 2006, Steve Groene made it official and asked Kootenai County Prosecutor Bill Douglas to stop his pursuit of the death penalty against Duncan. Groene expressed concern that a death penalty case would mean years of litigation, particularly in appeals were Duncan to be sentenced to death, if convicted. That would mean that Shasta would be forced to testify repeatedly over the years, for perhaps as long as two decades, before a death sentence would be imposed. The recurrence of Groene's throat cancer was another concern, bringing about fear that he may not live long enough to see the sentence carried out. Groene wants to be able to spend "quality time" with Shasta, but the fact that she would have to testify in a death penalty case could detract from that. Douglas indicated that he would carefully consider Groene's request, but that he would have to take into account the wishes of the family members of the other victims.

"It's too sudden for us to change course," Douglas said in a telephone interview with the Associated Press. "Right now our intent is to march on for the October 16, 2006, trial date. . . . My perspective is [that] nothing has changed. . . . My heart goes out to Steve. He feels he won't live long enough for the death penalty to be carried out. We will listen to what he has to say."

Steve McKenzie, victim Mark McKenzie's brother, does not want to see an agreement in which Duncan might consent to plead guilty in exchange for life in prison. Instead, McKenzie wants prosecutor Bill Douglas to continue his quest for the death penalty.

"The guy has spent most of his life in prison," McKenzie said recently. "To him, getting life in prison is like going home. . . . Brenda was real cool. Slade was a great kid. Everybody loved Dylan. My brother—he was my brother. I don't want to plea bargain."

According to Douglas, Brenda Groene's family is also supporting the death penalty for Duncan. Douglas indicated that it's his desire to hear from everybody in the family. Douglas indicated that dissension among the family members of the victims over whether to seek the death penalty or not has placed him in a difficult position—and Steve Groene's continuing battle with cancer also complicates things. He said that he speaks with Groene almost weekly.

"I pray for Steve's health every day, and for his entire family," Douglas said. "We feel very, very badly about his deteriorating health condition."

Nonetheless, "We will and still plan to call Shasta as an identification witness," Douglas told reporters recently, and she would likely have to face Duncan in court. Duncan has been charged with "very serious crimes that I have to prove beyond a reasonable doubt . . . it's our impression Shasta will help us in meeting that burden of proof . . . She's a critical, essential witness . . . the criminal justice system requires that even young victims must tell their story."

Douglas also expressed displeasure with those who speak out about the death penalty and argue that it is inappropriate regardless of the crime or crimes that have been committed.

"Those folks should have the guts to go to the state legislature," he said. "Otherwise, prosecutors like myself are obligated to apply Idaho law. Don't ask prosecutors to not apply it in cases like this. I'm obligated to carry out the law."

By May 2006, Steve Groene's request that the death penalty not be pursued against Duncan got the attention of federal prosecutors, prompting them to begin discussing a possible plea deal.

"The victims can be assured that we are listening carefully to them and are considering their wishes," said Marc Haus, an assistant U.S. Attorney in Boise. "We are also discussing their concerns with Kootenai County and the Department of Justice in Washington."

A Department of Justice official, who spoke on the condition of anonymity, confirmed to reporters that negotiations were indeed underway with Duncan's lawyers and were at a critical stage at the time of this writing (May 2006) despite the fact that other relatives of the victims want the death penalty for Duncan. Any deal made with Duncan, according to the official source, would most likely require that Duncan disclose details of other crimes that he has been alleged to have been involved in, such as the Anthony Martinez case in southern California and the slayings of Carmen Cubias and Sammiejo White in the Bothell, Washington, area.

Duncan's public defender, John Adams, indicated to reporters that Duncan might be willing to discuss a plea agreement if the possibility of the death penalty is removed from the scenario. Adams indicated that he believes Steve Groene's wishes would carry considerable weight in the prosecution's decision whether or not to continue pursuing the death penalty against Duncan.

"Steve Groene is a strong, mature adult," Adams said. "He is doing what he thinks is best for his family. That should be recognized."

JOSEPH EDWARD DUNCAN III IS CLEARLY A VIOLENT SEX OFfender who should have never seen the light of day following his conviction for raping the 14-year-old Tacoma boy in the woods at gunpoint. However, society must be careful in its zeal, in that it must find a way to separate the categorizing of violent offenders like Duncan, who are not amenable to treatment and should be locked away forever, from the harmless "hands off" perverts whose crimes, while damaging and hurtful to victims, can be eliminated by treatment programs that teach them how to stop offending. While there are no cures for sexually offensive behaviors, not even for the simple pervert, non-violent offenders can be taught techniques to control their urges and thus should somehow be governed under a separate system from that of the violent sex offender. Above all else, however, we should never lose sight of the victims and what they have been put through.

Joseph Edward Duncan III was originally scheduled to go to trial in April 2006 for the crimes he allegedly committed in northern Idaho and western Montana. However, his lawyers have successfully argued for a delay and Duncan is now scheduled to go to trial on October 16, 2006.

A hearing for pre-trial motions was scheduled for August 2006. Duncan's attorney, Public Defender John Adams, was planning to ask for a jury from outside Kootenai County to hear the case. Adams was also planning to ask the court to declare Idaho's 1982 repeal of the insanity defense as unconstitutional, an indication that he and his client might have been considering an insanity plea.

A new law passed in 2004 requires juries in death penalty cases to determine a defendant's fate. If Duncan is convicted of the killings for which he has been charged, it will be the first time in Kootenai County that a jury, as opposed to a judge, will be required to determine whether a defendant receives the death penalty. To date there have been only three death penalty cases in Idaho that have been tried under the new law, and juries imposed the death sentence in two of them.

The last time Kootenai County placed anyone on death row was in 1981, when Donald Paradis and Thomas Gibson were convicted of the strangulation death of 19-year-old Kimberly Palmer. Palmer's body was found in a creek in the Post Falls area. Paradis and Gibson were both released from prison when their convictions were overturned by an appeals court.

After Idaho's case against Duncan has concluded, federal prosecutors have said that it is likely that Duncan will be charged in federal court for the kidnapping of Shasta Groene, kidnapping and murder of Dylan Groene, and a variety of other crimes, including production of child pornography, presumably related to the videos he made of Shasta and Dylan while holding them in captivity.

It seems likely that Duncan will also eventually be charged in the murders of Sammiejo White and her sister Carmen Cubias, in which Duncan implicated himself, and with the abduction and murder of Anthony Martinez. Prosecutors in King County, Washington, which has jurisdiction in the White and Cubias case, would not comment on how that office might deal with Duncan. The Riverside County District Attorney's Office has said it is likely that Duncan will eventually be prosecuted there with regard to the Martinez case, but prosecutors have not decided whether they would seek the death penalty or not.

Meanwhile, the Coeur d'Alene School Board has reversed an earlier decision it had made to disallow a memorial plaque for Dylan Groene at Fernan Elementary School. The board members had been concerned that the plaque could further traumatize Shasta, who still attends the school and would have to face questions from other students about its presence. However, Steve Groene said that he had spoken with Shasta about the plaque, and she is in favor of it.

"I know Shasta would have no problem with it," Groene said. "She knows how much Dylan loves that school."

The plaque memorializing Dylan will be placed on the school's playground.

Another memorial for Dylan, consisting of three stone slabs, is nearly finished and will soon be placed at the Lolo National Forest campsite in Montana where he was killed.

JURY SELECTION WAS SCHEDULED TO BEGIN AT 9:00 A.M. ON Monday, October 16, 2006, for Joseph Edward Duncan's kidnapping and murder trial in Coeur d'Alene. However, there was much activity over the weekend between Kootenai County Prosecutor Bill Douglas and Duncan's defense attorney, Public Defender John Adams, which fueled speculation in the community that a deal was being worked out. As crowds gathered both inside and outside the Kootenai County courthouse anticipating what could have been classified as a "trial of the century," it quickly became obvious that a plea agreement had been reached.

Douglas presented 1st District Judge Fred Gibler with a stipulated facts document and informed the court that Duncan was ready to plead guilty to each of three counts of first-degree murder and three counts of first-degree kidnapping for causing the deaths of Brenda Kay Groene, Slade Vincent Groene, and Mark Edward McKenzie and for kidnapping Shasta and Dylan Groene for sexual purposes.

Duncan's stipulated agreement described how he had stalked the family for two days after selecting them at random when he saw Shasta playing outside her home in a bathing suit. According to the document, Duncan ordered Brenda to persuade Shasta and Dylan to cooperate with him. The document detailed how Slade had been struck 14 times with a claw hammer; Mark had been struck seven times and Brenda three times.

"This agreement is possible because of a brave little nine-year-old girl who was willing to confront Duncan face-to-face in the courtroom," Douglas told reporters.

"A lot of hard work went into this," Douglas added.

Duncan, clean-shaven and clothed in a button-down shirt and sweater, stood in front of the judge while Steve Groene and other family members watched from the gallery. After saying "guilty" six times, once for each of the charges, in front of Judge Gibler, Duncan was allowed to make a statement. He kept it brief.

"I've thought a lot about what I wanted to say," said Duncan. "I have nothing to say."

According to the deal, Duncan is required to cooperate with Kootenai County investigators working on the murder–kidnap aspect of the cases with regard to Shasta and Dylan. Furthermore, Duncan's guilty pleas cannot be withdrawn, and if he is not convicted in federal court, the state of Idaho can hold a death sentence trial in which Shasta would not be required to testify.

"Shasta will never be required to relive the events of 2005 in a courtroom," Douglas said. However, he said it appeared likely that she would be required to testify against Duncan in the federal case against him.

"Mr. Duncan wanted it to be known he entered into

this because he felt that the community and the families of the victim and especially Steve and Shasta Groene had been through enough," Adams said. "He didn't want to put them through any more."

Darlene Torres, Brenda's mother and Shasta's grandmother, told reporters that she didn't want to hear what Duncan's feelings were or what he had to say.

"It's like sitting in a room with the devil," Torres said. She expressed relief, however, that Shasta did not have to take the stand.

Duncan was sentenced to three consecutive life sentences without the possibility of parole.

According to U.S. Attorney Marc Haws, who will likely be the lead prosecutor in the federal case against Duncan, the federal charges are expected to include kidnapping, sexual abuse of Shasta and Dylan, child exploitation, and Dylan's murder. The Department of Justice has given approval for their prosecutors to seek the death penalty.

First, however, a federal grand jury will be called to hear the evidence against Duncan, which is expected to occur by early 2007.

"It's been a long, difficult road," Adams said. "I think for Kootenai County the case is over."

"We essentially gave up nothing," Douglas said. "It is virtually guaranteed he will face two death juries."

Steve Groene, unable to talk because of the removal of his larynx, held up a white placard with a handwritten message: "The Groene family wishes to thank everyone for their thoughts and prayers. We feel this is the best possible outcome."

—AFTERWORD—

My hope is that the story you have just read about sex offender, pedophile, kidnapper and murderer Joseph Edward Duncan III will raise your awareness about such human predators, and also do some good. I keep writing these books because readers frequently contact me through my web site, www.garycking.com, and tell me that my books do heighten their knowledge and understanding of the criminal mind, and they ask me to continue writing them. I've tried not to let them down, although it has been some time since I have written a book about a sex offender or a serial murderer. It is important to note that while all sex offenders do not become serial murderers, serial murderers are all too often sex offenders, particularly before their behavior escalates to the ultimate crime of murder, and in that sense they often come in pairs, as is the case in the story that you have just read.

Several years ago I wrote a book called *Driven to Kill*, about a sick, depraved young man named Westley Allan Dodd, a pedophile-turned-killer who preyed upon young boys to satisfy his unnatural desires. My motivation then, as it is now, was to raise public awareness about such anomalies of nature, to serve as a wake-up call of sorts in the hope that parents would take extra precautions with their greatest assets—their children—and do everything humanly possible to protect them, to keep them from becoming helpless victims of those whose sole drive is the fulfillment of their own perverted self-gratification.

With the publication of *Driven to Kill*, I, along with many others in various professions and walks of life, called on legislators across the country to implement tougher child predator and sex crime laws—and this was accomplished over time, apparently to little avail. Over the past decade or so, legislators at the federal, state and local levels have written and passed numerous new laws to be utilized in dealing with sex offenders, from indefinitely extending their prison time to following their movements after their release from prison.

However, despite everyone's best efforts, we still have as many sex offenders today, if not more, than we had in 1992, when the likes of Westley Allan Dodd terrorized the Pacific Northwest and caused parents to fear allowing their kids out of their houses to play. It appears that the tougher laws now in place, well meaning as they were, also served to personify the sex offender as a twenty-first-century bogeyman and may have actually done more harm than good—particularly with respect to the further erosion of civil rights in general.

Although one has to call into question whether or not sex offenders like Dodd or Duncan deserve any civil rights at all, we also have to question whether making a "bogeyman" out of these people to scare the rest of us into giving up *our* civil rights so that the sex offender's are diminished is really worth the cost. The latter was not my intention, as I'm sure it was not the intention of the honest lawmakers whose motives were not self-serving, but whose true interest lay in a sincere desire to keep these fiends locked away and off the streets, away from our children, where they belong. In the end, the cost of answering the question of whether sex offenders should ever have their civil rights restored is costing us all dearly.

Every era, however, has had its bogeyman, and politicians, particularly the self-serving ones, have used that bogeyman to further their own interests. Why should the twenty-first century be any different? While the tougher laws have helped to raise public awareness about sex offenders, they really haven't "solved" the problem of protecting ourselves and our loved ones from sexual predators. We still have sex offenders, we still have victims, and we still have fear of such individuals, albeit now immensely heightened. It now seems that the tougher laws have failed us as a society, and really have done little more than perform as a sounding board or a pulpit for those self-serving politicians seeking election by scaring us with the bogeyman. It now seems that the best protection of our children begins at home, and not on Capitol Hill.

Mothers and fathers everywhere simply need to spend more time teaching their children that there are people in the world who, through no fault of the child's, are bent on doing them harm. Educators in our country's classrooms could also find ways to integrate the subject matter into their classroom curricula and begin teaching children how not to become victims, and to provide education about fighting back or running away when confronted with potential harm from a stranger, or even from someone they know. Parents need to quit sending their youngsters to the store, on foot and alone, and instead do it themselves, and they should pay more attention when their children are playing outside in the yard. Even these types of precautions are sometimes not enough, as you have seen in the pages of the book you are now reading.

Although we certainly need many of the current laws in place, the tougher laws have helped pave the way for the erosion of our civil liberties through the degradation of the protections afforded by the Constitution—this, of course, was never anyone's intention, but the strong element of fear is at work here, and many of our politicians have skillfully used it against us to further their own agendas. Sex offender registration laws have, in essence, done little good in and of themselves. They have, of course, provided another sort of life sentence for those convicted of such crimes, despite the fact that they have paid their "debt to society" and have successfully completed sex offender treatment programs, but they have done little to protect us against the extremely dangerous type of offender like Duncan, the subject of this book.

The Duncans and Dodds of this world are the exception rather than the rule, and are very rare among the sex offender population. The majority of sex crimes committed today, eight out of ten in fact, are committed by relatives, friends or acquaintances, not by strangers. As we slowly awaken to this fact, we find that we are now beginning to question the constitutionality of the tougher laws that we urged our legislators to pass. This, in turn, has spawned a new fear, in that people are now beginning to wonder whether such a tough stance as publishing a registry of everyone who commits a sex crime might carry over to other types of crimes that we are less disgusted by or fearful of, crimes such as car theft, or burglary.

And what of the potential of spawning acts of vigilantism due to such registries?

According to *Preventing Sexual Violence: How Society Should Cope with Sex Offenders*, author and retired law professor John Q. LaFond uncovered numerous accounts of assaults and other crimes against sex offenders, in part because of the sex offender registry listings. It is tempting to dismiss that fact with a "Who cares?" But we need to begin questioning how we might feel if acts of vigilantism or harassment were to begin being committed against people convicted of any number of other non-sexual crimes because we as a society decided that we should place the names of *all* criminals in a public registry. Would that really solve the problem? Probably not.

It is a statistical fact that the recidivism rate among sex offenders is considerably lower than that of criminals who commit other crimes such as robbery, burglary, assault, drug offenses, murder and so forth, even though there is no "cure" for sex crime behavior. The recidivism rate among sex offenders, like Duncan and Dodd, except for the rarest, is approximately 13.4 percent, according to studies, while the rate among ex-convicts in general is approximately 66 percent—with most of these crimes committed within four years of parole! Studies show that this lower recidivism rate is likely due to the shame, embarrassment and humiliation that the sex offender undergoes during the initial conviction for his or her crimes. Studies have also shown that sex offender treatment programs, instead of providing "cures," do provide the offender with behavior modification techniques that can be used to "turn off" or shut down the urge to offend when it occurs, and prevent future crimes.

LaFond, in an interview with Crime Library, said that the current methods of dealing with sex offenders by placing them on registries is a waste of public resources, money that could be used to supervise and provide behavior-modifying treatment for those offenders who are deemed the most threatening.

"Our current policies assume that all sex offenders are equally dangerous," LaFond told Crime Library, "and that one size fits all in their treatment and monitoring. We box up large numbers of sex offenders for long periods of time, but ultimately we release those same [dangerous] sex offenders back into the community with minimal supervision and control."

Instead, says LaFond, we try to control the sex offender through the current registry system, which does little more than place the burden on society to take matters into their own hands. This, LaFond suggests, also promotes vigilantism.

"It's almost as though the state is saying, 'There's a dangerous sex offender living within your midst. We have done all we can; the rest is up to you,' " LaFond said.

As a society we must, therefore, ask ourselves, is justice being served when we decide to impose a life sentence on one type of criminal, a fate that knows no end, when we at the same time allow other types of criminals

who typically have higher recidivism rates to go free after they've "paid their debt to society"?

Many of these sex offenders must re-register with local law enforcement year after year for the rest of their
lives, while the Duncans and Dodds of this world somehow slip through the cracks of that system. Aren't the
Duncans and Dodds the ones that should never see the
light of day again? Have we gone so far in our efforts to
curb crime of all sorts that we've paid little mind that we
are doing away with our civil liberties in the process, all
because of our willingness to allow our politicians to
maximize their own agendas by playing on our fears?

These are complicated questions to which there are
no easy answers. Because this book's subject matter
evokes strong fear and revulsion, which propel us as a
society to take drastic measures to protect ourselves and
our loved ones, we don't think clearly about the answers
until we look backward. It therefore seems appropriate
to address them here, even if only on the surface.

Most people don't feel comfortable knowing that
they have a sex offender living in their neighborhood,
and rightly so. However, would they feel any less appre-
hensive if a murderer lived two doors down? Probably
not. Under today's laws, lists and databases will tell us
about the sex offender, but a paroled murderer can live
next door and we wouldn't necessarily know about it unless the murderer had also committed a sex crime. It
seems like there's something wrong with this picture.
Perhaps we should employ the same laws that apply to
sex criminals across the board by having all criminals
register for life and place their information into local,
state and national databases that the public can access?

But as tempting as it may be, do we jeopardize our civil liberties along with the criminal's?

And while we're at it, shouldn't we also include juvenile offenders? Just because a kid is underage is no reason to protect his identity, is it? Kids can be vicious and dangerous, and could just as easily kill me or a loved one as an adult could. I've written about some of those types as well. Alex and Derek King (no relation to yours truly), who killed their father with a baseball bat and set his house on fire to cover up their crime, are prime examples. I would want to know if either of those two boys lived in my neighborhood after their release from prison.

Given the fact that sex offenders have become the bogeyman of the twenty-first century, we know about them living in our neighborhoods before we know about other classifications of criminals. A terrorist may very well be living down the street awaiting orders from al-Qaeda and Osama bin Laden (another modern-day bogeyman used here as an example, albeit an extreme one, to stress the point of how our politicians sometimes work against those of us who still believe in the freedom and values that our Founding Fathers provided—such believers in, and defenders of, freedom were once called patriots).

So what are we to do? How do we protect ourselves from criminals such as sex offenders without undoing some of the well-meaning laws that are now in place, and without trampling all over our Constitution and civil liberties in the process? It's not going to be easy to find solutions to these and other problems facing us today, particularly in a political climate like that in which we now live, where the push is on to scare people into giving up their freedom for security.

My point in going on so about this is not to argue the case of the sex offender; quite the contrary. We need to know when such people are in our midst, just as we need to know when a murderer or a thief is among us. But we need to put our need to know into the proper perspective, i.e., do I really need to know that Bob Smith, who molested his cousin when he was a teenager, lives down the block?

People like the subject of this book, Joseph Edward Duncan III, do not make it any easier to intelligently discuss such a delicate subject matter. Clearly we need to know about people like Duncan, whose insatiable appetite for depraved sex, rape and murder has allegedly compelled him to commit crime after crime and who would no doubt have gone on and on had he not been stopped. But we also have to ask ourselves whether we have gone too far in the eradication of our own civil liberties by allowing, even encouraging, our legislators to create and enact laws from which there is no return.

It is easy to be a staunch supporter of the death penalty—unless you are the person who has been sentenced to die and you did not commit the crime. How many times in the last decade has an innocent person on death row been cleared of the crime of murder through DNA analysis after serving years awaiting a fate that was not deserved and, thankfully, did not occur? There are many cases that can be recounted, in many different states. How many innocent people who were sentenced to death weren't fortunate enough to have escaped the executioner's needle because they had not been cleared through DNA analysis or in some other way, and wrongly met the permanent fate of death? One person, in this writer's opinion, would be one person too many.

Think, for a moment, by putting yourselves into the shoes of a loved one, a relative or close family member of someone who was wrongly put to death—how would you feel if you knew that that person was innocent? And consider how such a blunder of justice would affect a victim's family, knowing that the wrong person had been executed for the murder of their loved one and that the real killer was still out there somewhere?

Clearly, law enforcement needs to know where sex offenders, rapists, murderers and criminals of all sorts are, at any given time. But do we need a system in place that sometimes works like a formula to instigate vigilantism, as was seen in the pages of this book when we explored the case of a Seattle area man who killed two sex offenders after Duncan's crime spree? There clearly are no easy answers to this dilemma—we seem damned if we do and damned if we don't. However, Benjamin Franklin may have said it best: "Those who would give up essential liberty to purchase a little temporary safety, deserve neither liberty nor safety."

Sex offenders are not some new phenomenon that appeared in our midst overnight. They have been around since time began, likely in the same numbers proportionate to the population at any given time in history. However, our perception and fear of such abnormal people is relatively new, due in large part to the tragic cases of Megan Kanka, Polly Klaas, Jacob Wetterling, Adam Walsh, Lee Joseph Iseli, Billy and Cole Neer and now, Dylan and Shasta Groene, to name but a few.

It is questionable, even doubtful, that any of the treatment programs that exist, both inside and outside of prison, could have helped the likes of Duncan. Even though there are programs that have been shown to help some offenders accept responsibility for their crimes, it is doubtful that such a program could have benefited Joseph Edward Duncan III. It is a sad fact that some people cannot be helped. Duncan, you will recall, had a chance to receive help in such a program while he was a teenager, but blew it when he chose to peep into windows while supposedly out on a pass visiting his mother. It is highly doubtful that people like Duncan could ever be taught the methods needed to control deviant sexual urges and develop relapse prevention skills.

The toughest, most stringent laws that mankind is capable of thinking up and getting placed on the books will clearly not stop the Dodds and Duncans of this world, any more than vigilantism will. They will simply continue to exist and will have to be dealt with accordingly, probably after their crime spree has been stopped by their capture or their death.

Such perverts have always existed, and they always will. However, through heightened awareness of who sex offenders are, where they come from, and what creates them, we can learn how to better protect ourselves and our children from such scum without taking our laws to the extreme where they only serve to diminish our own civil liberties and Constitutional protections.

Once we have destroyed the gifts of our Founding Fathers in the name of fear, they will be next to impossible to replace.

But then, what are we to do?

APPENDIX
Joseph Edward Duncan III Timeline

February 25, 1963—Joseph Edward Duncan III is born in Tacoma, Washington, to Joseph E. Duncan Jr. and Lillian Mae Duncan, according to the Associated Press; an MSNBC report claims that Duncan was born at Fort Bragg, North Carolina; a prison psychological evaluation dated March 16, 2000, says that he was born in New Orleans, Louisiana.

1971—Experiences first sexual contact at the age of 8, initiated by two young female relatives.

1975—Sexually assaults a 5-year-old boy at age 12, according to what Duncan told therapists later in life.

1978—At 15, Duncan rapes a 9-year-old boy at gunpoint.

1979—After engaging police in a high-speed chase while driving a stolen vehicle at age 15, Duncan attempts to run through a roadblock and crashes the car. The crash damages the right side of his face, requiring surgery, and he is sent to Dyslin's boys' ranch in Tacoma, Washington, where he tells a therapist that he has bound and sexually assaulted six boys and estimates that he has committed thirteen rapes of young boys.

1980—Duncan is sentenced to prison for raping a 14-year-old boy at gunpoint in Tacoma, Washington.

May 19, 1980—Duncan is court-ordered to undergo psychological and medical testing, as well as treatment, at Western State Hospital. The following day he is sent to the hospital's Mentally Ill Offender Program.

March 1982—After twenty-two months in a sex offender program, therapists decide that Duncan is not trying to make his treatment work, due to his activities of window-peeping and masturbating while out on pass to visit relatives. He is subsequently transferred to the Department of Corrections to serve out the remainder of his prison term.

June 1984—Duncan is placed into protective custody because other inmates are pressuring him for sex.

April 1985—Duncan is moved into "preferred housing" with greater freedom of movement.

May 1987—An Indeterminate Sentence Review Board finds that Duncan is capable of making parole. However, because of a number of serious infractions, his parole is actually still several years away.

January 1989—Duncan is determined by Parole Board to be a high-risk to re-offend. Specialized treatment and close supervision are recommended.

March 1989—Duncan is now two years beyond his original release date. Under a transition program, he cannot find acceptable parole resources in which to live and work and is therefore denied parole.

April 1989—Duncan is transferred to a facility where his behavior can be more closely monitored in an open setting.

November 1989—Duncan tells parole board members that he has decided to begin exploring his feminine traits.

January 1991—Duncan begins a pen-pal relationship with a King County revenue officer, David Woelfert.

April 1991—Items of Duncan's mail are withheld after determining that publications he was attempting to have sent to him clearly depict child pornography.

April 1992—Duncan is found ineligible for parole and an additional 36 months is added to his prison term under the provisions of the State of Washington indeterminate sentencing guidelines for sex offenders.

June 1992—Duncan requests his court records because of the additional years added to his prison term.

July 1992—The parole board reverses its decision of finding Duncan ineligible for parole.

April 1993—Duncan tries to involve his friend, David Woelfert, in his attempts to alter an official document to misrepresent the seriousness of his crimes. He is caught and receives a serious reprimand for the infraction.

May 1993—Duncan receives administrative segregation because of his fear that other inmates will pressure him for sex, thus causing him to resist and fight back. Duncan told the parole board that he would not resist because he does not want to receive additional infractions for fighting because of his desire to make parole.

September 1994—Duncan, 31, is released on parole to a halfway house in Seattle after serving 14 years in prison.

November 1994—Duncan undergoes routine urinalysis as a condition of his parole and tests positive for amphetamines. He blames the positive reaction on over-the-counter cold medications, receives warning.

January 1996—Duncan informs his parole officer that he is exploring a relationship with a woman who is married and has two small children. He explains that she is helping him explore his "feminine side" by assisting him with his transsexual fantasies. He begins buying and wearing women's clothing.

April 1996—Duncan's therapist takes him on a gay retreat to Leavenworth, Washington, to observe how he deals with other gay men.

July 1996—Sammiejo White, 11, and her half sister, Carmen Cubias, 9, are last seen leaving a Seattle motel room.

October 1996—Duncan violates his parole for marijuana use and possession of a firearm. He spends 30 days in jail and is released.

November 1996—Duncan tells his parole officer that he intends to give up homosexuality for a heterosexual lifestyle.

March 1997—Duncan tests positive, again, for marijuana use. He violates at least nine conditions of his parole, including having contact with minor children in Seattle and moving without receiving permission from his parole officer. He is ordered to undergo a polygraph examination in Seattle on March 26, 1997, which he fails with regard to his interaction with children. His last communication with his parole officer occurs on March 27.

March 26, 1997—Deborah Palmer, 7, is last seen walking to school in Oak Harbor, Washington. Her body washes up on a beach five days later, on March 31. Duncan was known to be in that area on the date the girl disappeared.

March 31, 1997—Duncan steals his girlfriend's 1986 Chrysler New Yorker and disappears. His mother tells his parole officer that she last saw him on March 31 and has no idea where he might have gone.

April 4, 1997—Anthony Martinez, 10, is kidnapped by a man with a mustache in Beaumont, California. The boy's body is found two weeks later, on April 19, in the desert, bound with duct tape and partially buried. A partial fingerprint is found on duct tape. It would take nine years, but the fingerprint would eventually be identified as Duncan's.

August 1997—Duncan is arrested by the FBI at his half sister's house in Kansas City, Missouri, for failing to register as a sex offender. He is returned to prison in Washington.

December 1997—Two inmates file complaints against Duncan, claiming that he propositioned them for sex. They said that when they refused his advances he became irritable, angry, and made threatening remarks to them.

February 1998—The remains of Sammiejo White and Carmen Cubias are found on a farm near Bothell, Washington.

July 2000—After receiving letters of support from various individuals declaring that he is not a threat to society, Duncan is released from prison without parole or probation. His only requirement is that he register as a sex offender. Later that month he relocates to Fargo, North Dakota, and registers with the local police department. He is classified as a Level III sex offender, the highest of the rating tiers, indicative that he is among those most likely to re-offend.

September 2000—Enrolls at North Dakota State University majoring in computer programming. Makes the dean's list for both the fall 2000 and spring 2001 semesters.

April 2001—Begins going by the name Jet, or Jazzi-Jet, and sets up a gay website. Photos on the site depict him as a cross-dresser.

June 2003—Leanna "Beaner" Warner disappears from her home in Chisholm, Minnesota, approximately 200 miles from Fargo.

October 2003—Duncan receives a visit from three Fargo police officers, who question him about harassing women in town.

January 2004—Begins a new website called "Blogging the Fifth Nail." He discusses Leanna Warner in his first post. Blog is focused on his perception of unfair treatment of sex offenders.

July 2004—Duncan travels to Detroit Lakes, Minnesota, in Becker County, where he molests one boy and tries to molest another at a school playground.

February, 2005—Two days before his 42nd birthday, Duncan receives a summons to appear in Becker County, Minnesota. He is subsequently charged with second-degree criminal sexual conduct and second-degree attempted sexual conduct in connection with the July 2004 incident involving the two young boys.

April 5, 2005—Duncan posts bail in Becker County with borrowed money and is released.

April 11, 2005—Duncan's last contact with Fargo police. He leaves the area after purchasing night-vision goggles, and subsequently rents a 2005 red Jeep Grand Cherokee in St. Paul, Minnesota.

April 27, 2005—Duncan allegedly steals license plates off of a vehicle in Newton County, Missouri, and places them on the Jeep.

May 4, 2005—The Jeep is reported stolen after Duncan fails to return it.

May 6, 2005—An arrest warrant is issued for Duncan when he fails to show up for a scheduled court appearance in Minnesota.

Mid-May, 2005—Duncan arrives in Idaho and allegedly begins stalking the Groene family home outside Coeur d'Alene for several days.

May 15, 2005—Mark McKenzie and members of the Groene family are last seen alive at a barbecue at their home. An intruder binds and kills three members of the family sometime on May 15–16, and kidnaps Shasta and Dylan Groene.

July 2, 2005—Shasta Groene is found with Duncan at a Denny's restaurant in Coeur d'Alene after staff and customers recognize her. Duncan is arrested.

July 4, 2005—Remains are found at a remote campsite in western Montana and are believed to be those of Dylan Groene.

July 8, 2005—Police determine that a hammer was used to kill Brenda Groene, Slade Groene, and Mark McKenzie.

July 10, 2005—Dylan Groene's remains are positively identified.

July 12, 2005—Duncan is charged with first-degree murder in the deaths of Brenda and Slade Groene and Mark McKenzie.

July 14, 2005—Duncan mentions the name Martinez during an interview with detectives, which leads to his fingerprint being identified on the duct tape found on Anthony Martinez's body. Duncan also implicates himself in the abductions and murders of Sammiejo White and Carmen Cubias.

June 2006—Duncan has "lawyered up" and has not spoken to detectives on the advice of his attorney.

October 2006—Duncan pleads guilty to three counts of first-degree murder and to three counts of first-degree kidnapping in the murders of Brenda and Slade Groene and Mark McKenzie, and the abductions of Shasta and Dylan Groene. He is sentenced to three consecutive life terms.